FROM AIRBUS
TO ZEPPELIN

FROM **A**IRBUS

TO **Z**EPPELIN

FACTS, FIGURES AND QUOTES FROM THE WORLD OF AVIATION

Norman Ferguson

Front cover: Airbus A380 go around/aborted
landing at 'Internationalen Luftfahrtausstellung
Berlin 2006' (Tino 'Scorpi' Keitel, Bearbeiter:
Johann H. Addicks via Wikimedia Commons)
People watching the landing of Zeppelin LZ 127.
(Grombo via Wikimedia Creative Commons)

Back cover: *Atlantis* on Shuttle Carrier Aircraft.
(NASA/Carla Thomas)

First published 2016

The History Press
The Mill, Brimscombe Port
Stroud, Gloucestershire, GL5 2QG
www.thehistorypress.co.uk

© Norman Ferguson, 2016

The right of Norman Ferguson to be identified as the Author
of this work has been asserted in accordance with the
Copyright, Designs and Patents Act 1988.

British Library Cataloguing in Publication Data.
A catalogue record for this book is available from the British Library.

ISBN 978 0 7509 6838 6

Typesetting and origination by The History Press
Printed and bound in Great Britain by TJ International Ltd

INTRODUCTION

When the Wright Brothers took to the air in December 1903, and Count von Zeppelin created the world's first airline six years later, they could have had little idea of how quickly the aviation industry would grow to become the global transportation supplier that is a part of so many of our everyday lives.

The first powered aircraft could only go in straight lines, they suffered control and stability problems and could only fly in favourable weather conditions, but soon all these issues were overcome as experimentation produced better machines. They went faster, higher and further, being pushed on by competitive individuals and the commercial gains to be made. Eventually, they could fly high enough to earn their pilots astronaut wings. Aircraft grew in size from the wood and canvas structures of the first years of flight to the current giant Antonov An-225 transport, with a cargo bay 20ft longer than the Wright Brothers' first flight.

Aircraft were used for a multitude of tasks: hauling cargo, carrying passengers, mapping the Earth below, rescuing downed flyers, researching the atmosphere, entertaining astounded audiences and of course in warfare, with machines able to carry weapons of unimaginable destruction.

With so many aspects to aviation and its history, an A–Z is an ideal way of presenting them (or at least some of them). To give an idea of the breadth of this subject, the first chapter includes the worst airship disasters: ace-in-a-day fighter pilot Jorma Sarvanto, an early accident at Juvisy in 1909, an account of an aerobatic display by Douglas Bader, details of the world's first double-decker jet airliner the Airbus A380, and the flying career of the remarkable Amy Johnson.

Norman Ferguson
Summer 2016

ACKNOWLEDGEMENTS

Special thanks go to:

Chrissy McMorris and Amy Rigg at The History Press for making the creation of *From Airbus to Zeppelin* such a pleasant and professional experience. Edinburgh City Council libraries for that great idea of free books to take home. Robert Prest for allowing the inclusion of an excerpt from his masterful book on the F-4 Phantom. And especially to my family for their continued help and support (and the free books).

ACCIDENT AT JUVISY

At 5 o'clock the aviator M. Blanck in a Bleriot monoplane started from the aerodrome, but after he had risen to the height of the grand stand something appeared to have happened to his steering apparatus and the aeroplane dashed into the middle of the public, causing great consternation. The screw was broken into fragments, which flew in all directions. Three persons, including two ladies, were hurt.

The Times, 19 October 1909

This unfortunate event took place during the aviation meet called the *Grande Quinzaine d'Aviation* (Great Fortnight of Aviation) held at Juvisy outside Paris. One of the injured sued the organisers for compensation but judges decreed that as aviation was a dangerous business and there were no regulations for such events it was at the attendee's risk. During the event the aviator Comte de Lambert flew his Wright biplane over the Eiffel Tower, a feat that caused much excitement.[1]

ACE-IN-A-DAY

The 1939 to 1940 Soviet–Finnish 'Winter War' is often forgotten, but one man's aerial combat achievements deserve to be remembered. Jorma Sarvanto was a Finnish fighter pilot who on 6 January 1940 achieved a remarkable record by shooting down six enemy aircraft. He would have downed more but ran out of ammunition. His targets were part of a formation of eight Soviet Ilyushin DB.3 bombers that had attacked the city of Kuopio. They had already lost one of their aircraft to another Finn, Per-Erik Sovelius, when they were attacked by the lone Fokker D.XXI fighter flown by Sarvanto.[2]

ADOLPHE PÉGOUD

In September 1913 the French aviator Adolphe Pégoud gained much acclaim by flying manoeuvres not seen publicly before. At the end of that month he came to the United Kingdom where he performed over three days at Brooklands.

In a Bleriot monoplane, Pégoud demonstrated several aerobatic manoeuvres which while now are commonplace, were sensational to the onlooking public and press at the time.

Flight Magazine called his flying 'phenomenal' and Pégoud's mastery in performing a loop was described in *The Times* newspaper under the headline 'The New Flying' the following day:

> At 4.45 Pégoud was off again, this time to 'loop the loop'. He now climbed to about 4,500 feet and at 5.05, amid a great silence, dived until he was again inverted, and in this attitude performed a spiral volplane, concluding with an 'S' as before. On this occasion he must have been hanging head downwards for nearly three-quarters of a minute. Resuming his flight, he climbed again for a few moments, then the machine dived, carried on, stood up on its tail, carried on upside down, and dived again, completing the full circle. A quick descent brought Pégoud's performance to a close. Another scene of enthusiasm followed, while his compatriots kissed him.
>
> *The Times*, 26 September 1913

Pégoud became the first ace in the First World War but was shot down and killed in 1915.

AEROBATIC TEAMS

The RAF had given formation aerobatic displays before the Second World War and continued these aerial exhibitions of piloting skills in peacetime. In the 1950s named aerobatic teams appeared for the first time. They were flown by flying training units or occasionally by operational squadrons until the 1970s. Cost-cutting saw the gradual decline of such flying and now the RAF has only one jet aerobatic team.

RAF Aerobatic Teams and their aircraft 1950s–1970s[3]

Gemini Pair (BAC Jet Provost)
Linton GIN (BAC Jet Provost)
The Black Arrows (Hawker Hunter)
The Black Knights (Hawker Hunter)
The Blades (BAC Jet Provost)
The Blue Chips (de Havilland Chipmunk)
The Blue Diamonds (Hawker Hunter)

The Bulldogs (Scottish Aviation Bulldog)
The Cranwell Poachers (BAC Jet Provost)
The Falcons (Hawker Hunter)
The Fighting Cocks (Hawker Hunter)
The Firebirds (English Electric Lightning)
The Gazelles (Aérospatiale Gazelle)
The Gin Four (BAC Jet Provost)
The Macaws (BAC Jet Provost)
The Magistrates (BAC Jet Provost)
The Meteorites (Gloster Meteor)
The Pelicans (BAC Jet Provost)
The Pelicans (Gloster Meteor)
The Poachers (BAC Jet Provost)
The Red Arrows (Folland Gnat)
The Red Pelicans (BAC Jet Provost)
The Redskins (BAC Jet Provost)
The Skylarks (de Havilland Chipmunk)
The Sparrows (Hunting Provost/BAC Jet Provost)
The Swords (BAC Jet Provost)
The Tigers (English Electric Lightning)
The Tomahawks (Agusta Bell Sioux)
The Vipers (BAC Jet Provost)
The Yellowjacks (Folland Gnat)

AEROBATICS

There came a demonstration of combined aerobatics by Flight Lieutenant H.M.A. Day and Pilot Officer D.R.S. Bader, both of No. 23 (Fighter) Squadron, flying Gamecocks. This was without any doubt the finest exhibition we have ever seen. Their timing was perfect and their showmanship really good. They managed to keep well up wind and did not gradually drift across the aerodrome in the way we have so often seen, and were at all times just the right height to be seen comfortably. Particularly spectacular was their method of flying off up the aerodrome side-by-side after having done a dive and rocket opposing each other. This was accomplished by an aileron turn inwards while nose down after the rocket. The display was doubly interesting in that it was probably the last time these Gamecocks would be seen in public, as we were told that they had been kept on charge in the squadron, which has since been equipped with Bulldogs, solely for this display.

This was a report of a display organised by the Newcastle-upon-Tyne Aero Club in *Flight* magazine on 28 August 1931. Three months later Douglas Bader was practising aerobatics in a Bulldog, at a lower altitude than was advised, when his wingtip caught the ground and he crashed. Although he survived, both legs were amputated. Despite this he returned to RAF operational flying and commanded a fighter squadron during the Battle of Britain.

AIRBUS A380

In the 1960s, Britain, France and Germany formed Airbus to build airliners capable of competing with the large US manufacturers such as Boeing. The first aircraft built was the A300, which made its maiden flight in 1972 and went into service two years later. Other types were built such as the four-engined A340 and best-selling two-engined A320.

In 2003 Airbus reached a milestone when it passed Boeing in the number of aircraft delivered. By the end of 2015 it had sold over 16,000 aircraft. That year it opened its first factory in the USA.

In the 1980s plans were devised to make an aircraft able to compete with Boeing's 747, its famous four-engined 'jumbo jet'. The result was the A380, the world's first twin-deck and twin-aisle airliner. The world's largest airliner made its first flight on 27 April 2005.

Emirates Airbus A380 approaching Manchester Airport. (Norman Ferguson)

A380 in facts and figures

0.89	Maximum Mach number
22	Undercarriage wheels
79	Height (ft)
130	Speed of toilet flush (mph)
220	Number of cabin windows
261	Wingspan (ft)
330	Length of cabling (miles)
853	Maximum passengers
8,200	Range (nautical miles)
77,000	Thrust per engine (lb)
84,600	Fuel capacity (US gallons)
1,268,000	Maximum take off weight (lb)
432,600,000	Average list price (US dollars)

The aircraft suffered delays going into service as it was discovered during installation that the aircraft's cabin cabling was too short. With miles of wiring inside the aircraft this presented a major problem.

As Airbus is a collaborative venture, its partner countries each make component parts, which are then assembled to form the final aircraft. The cause of the short cabling was put down to different versions of software used by German and French facilities. Each version worked out the amount of cabling required to bend around corners in a different way. It was this incompatibility that resulted in months of delay and billions of euros lost.

The A380 entered service in October 2007 with Singapore Airlines. Up until December 2015, 319 had been ordered.[4]

AIRSHIP DISASTERS

In the early years of the twentieth century airships were the main method of carrying aerial passengers, but as with other methods of human flight, there were inherent risks. While thousands of miles were flown safely, an airship's loss could be a spectacular and potentially disastrous event. The major non-wartime airship losses were:

Airship	Date	Country of Origin	Details	Casualties/ Survivors
LZ 18/ (L.2 navy designation)	17 October 1913	Germany	Caught fire and exploded when leaking hydrogen was ignited by one of the engines.	28 killed

Airship L.2 falls in flames.
(Library of Congress, Prints
& Photographs Division
LC-USZ62-74678)

R.38/ZR-2 (US Navy designation)	24 August 1921	UK	While being tested before handed over to US Navy, crashed into River Humber after structural failure.	44 killed, 5 survived
Roma	21 February 1922	USA	Crashed at Norfolk, Virginia, after loss of control sent it towards power lines and it burst into flames.	34 killed, 12 survived
Dixmude	21 December 1923	Germany/ France	The LZ 114 was given to France as war reparation. Exploded over Mediterranean Sea.	52 killed
ZR-1 *Shenandoah*	3 September 1925	USA	Crashed during a thunderstorm when winds were too strong for its structure.	13 killed, 29 survived
R101	5 October 1930	UK	Leaking gasbag caused loss of lift. Crashed in France.	48 killed, 6 survivors

ZRS-4 *Akron*	4 April 1933	USA	Lost in a thunderstorm off New Jersey. A previous airship named *Akron* had exploded in 1912, killing all five on board.	73 killed, 3 survivors
ZRS-5 *Macon*	12 February 1935	USA	Lost at sea off Point Sur, California, during a storm when upper fin failed and gasbag was punctured.	2 killed, 74 survived
Hindenburg	6 May 1937	Germany	Burst into flames while mooring.	36 killed, 62 survived

AMY JOHNSON

The foremost British female pilot of the 'Golden Age' was undoubtedly Amy Johnson, who earned her place in aviation history by becoming the first woman to fly solo to Australia in 1930.

Johnson, who was 26 years old, was attempting to break Bert Hinkler's record of sixteen days but failed, her journey taking twenty days. She was delayed by having to have repairs carried out on her plane, the small de Havilland Gipsy Moth biplane *Jason*, and having to land in the desert on the way to Baghdad due to bad visibility and strong winds.

Amy Johnson's Route to Australia

Day	Overnight Stop	Daily Distance travelled (miles)
1	Vienna	775
2	Constantinople	800
3	Aleppo	575
4	Baghdad	460
5	Bandar Abbas	850
6	Karachi	700
7	Jhansi	750
8	Calcutta	650
9	Rangoon	650
10	Rangoon	-
11	Rangoon	-
12	Bangkok	350
13	Singora	450
14	Singapore	465

15	Tjomal	760
16	Sourabaya	240
17	Sourabaya	-
18	Atamboea (Timor)	925
19	Atamboea (Timor)	-
20	Port Darwin	485

Her achievement was made all the more remarkable as she had never made a long-distance flight before setting off (her longest flight before was from London to her hometown of Hull) and she had less than 100 hours flying time. These epic distances were achieved in an aircraft with a maximum speed of 90mph.

Both the press and the public fêted her, when she arrived back in Britain. At a luncheon given in her honour at the Savoy in London, among the guests were pioneers Louis Blériot, Arthur Whitten Brown and Claude Graham-White as well as the writer Noel Coward and songwriter Ivor Novello.

Johnson flew several other long-distance flights including:

Departure	Destination	Year	Aircraft	Co-pilot/ engineer	Notes
UK (Lympne)	Japan	1931	DH.80A Puss Moth *Jason II*	Jack Humphreys	Journey included first one-day flight from UK to Moscow.
UK (Lympne)	Cape Town, South Africa	1932	DH.80A Puss Moth *Desert Cloud*	(Solo)	Set new record, beating that of husband Jim Mollison, also set a record on the return journey.
UK (Pendine Sands, South Wales)	New York, USA	1933	DH.84 Dragon *Seafarer*	Jim Mollison	Intended record flight failed with a crash-landing in Connecticut after low fuel made them abandon reaching New York.
UK (Mildenhall, Suffolk)	Australia	1934	DH.88 Comet *Black Magic*	Jim Mollison	Failed attempt to win MacRobertson Air Race but did set a record time to India.
Gravesend, UK	Cape Town, South Africa	1936	Percival Gull Six	(Solo)	Set new record. Last long-distance flight.

Johnson joined the Air Transport Auxiliary in 1940, but died in January 1941 after bailing out of an Airspeed Oxford over the Thames Estuary.[5]

AUCTION

At an auction in July 2015 Spitfire Mk1 P9374 sold for £3.1 million. The fighter had been painstakingly restored after being recovered from the beach at Calais where it had lain in the sands since crash-landing in 1940. Part of the money from the sale went to the Royal Air Force Benevolent Fund.

B IS FOR...

B-52 BAIL OUT

Getting out of a stricken aircraft has always presented problems to aircrew. In the First World War, pilots and observers were not generally issued with parachutes and had to crash-land their machines or die in them. Some pilots carried pistols in case their aircraft caught fire and they were unable to escape in time. In the Second World War, aircrew had parachutes but with enclosed canopies had lost the advantage of escaping more easily from their predecessors' open cockpits. In bomber aircraft they had to make their way to small hatches to jump out – made all the more difficult in the dark in aircraft often on fire.

As aircraft speeds increased, ejector seats were developed and these provided an effective way of having crew escape, although a mixture of the old and the new technologies lived side-by-side in 1950s aircraft like the B-52 Stratofortress. The pilot, co-pilot and electronic warfare officer had ejection seats (upwards firing) while the two navigators who sat on a

B-52 in flight. (USAF/Master Sgt Kevin Gruenwald)

lower deck had to eject downwards, which was suited more for high-level egress than low-level. The gunner in the early marks of the bomber sat on his own at the rear of the aircraft, below the tail fin, and had to jettison his turret before escaping.

The procedures for the gunner were laid out as follows:

Gunner's Bailout Procedure
1. Fasten safety belt, shoulder harness, oxygen mask and chin strap. Helmet visor down.
2. Pull up turret-drag chute interconnect knob upon pilot command only.
3. Pull jettison handle on pilot's command. Notify pilot ready to bailout.
4. Pull bailout bottle release cord.
5. Unfasten safety belt. WARNING: Pull integrated harness release handle only when using modified B-5 parachute.
6. Leave the airplane with arms and legs held close to body.
7. Pull parachute arming lanyard knob.

Bailout From Right Rear Wheel Well

Airspeed 275 knots (Indicated Air Speed) or less. If turret does not jettison request pilot to lower right aft landing gear – follow alternate bailout procedure.

The tail gunner was later given a seat next to the other crew and operated the guns remotely.[6]

BEAUTIFUL AIRCRAFT

Aircraft are not specifically designed to be beautiful but to fulfil a function. If beauty is in the eye of the beholder then what makes a beautiful aircraft is as subjective as any oil painting or a sculpture.

The choices here are based on a combination of balance, poise and other unquantifiable elements that create an object proving the adage 'if it looks right it'll fly right'.

Concorde

The fact that Concorde is thought of as a graceful machine, despite the brute strength of its four reheated Olympus engines, shows the sheer beauty of its design. Many delta-winged aircraft are attractive shapes but

Concorde's long and thin fuselage, set within two gently curving delta wings, makes it number one.

de Havilland Comet

de Havilland's next Comet was the world's first jet airliner. Its beauty stems from its sleek lines unencumbered by engines that were embedded into the wings, close to the fuselage. Its broad wings were swept back and the whole design was well balanced.

de Havilland DH.88 Comet

The 1930s saw many gorgeous looking aircraft, but the DH.88 was perhaps the best of them all. The twin-engine monoplane was built for speed, to take part in the UK to Australia MacRobertson Air Race of 1934. Needless to say it won. The winning machine, *Grosvenor House*, was painted in a bright red and white scheme, which added to its attractiveness.

Hawker Hunter

The Hunter derived from a specification for a high-level interceptor with an additional ground-attack role and first flew in 1951. Its single engine, mid-set swept wings, thin fuselage and swept-back tail planes mirroring the tail fin in shape, all combined to produce Britain's finest looking fighter of the decade.

Lockheed Constellation

The 'Connie' would face few dissenting voices as to its physical appearance. Its long, subtly curved fuselage, finished with triple tail fins, sets it out as one of the most appealing airliners ever built.

BISMARCK

The Air Ministry published *We Speak From the Air – Broadcasts by the RAF* in 1942. It featured select transcripts of radio broadcasts made by serving RAF personnel. These ranged from night fighter pilots recounting their successes against German bombers attacking London to accounts of low-level raids on occupied Europe.

One of the broadcasts – the speakers were kept anonymous – entitled 'We Shadowed the *Bismarck*' – tells of how a Coastal Command Catalina flying boat tracked down and was then spotted itself by the renowned German battleship *Bismarck*.

> As first, as we weren't sure that it was an enemy battleship, we had to make certain. So we altered course, went up to about 1,500ft into a cloud and circled. We thought we were near the stern of her when the cloud ended and there we were, right above her. The first we knew of it was a couple of puffs of smoke just outside the cockpit window, and a devil of a lot of noise. And then we were surrounded by dark brownish black smoke as she pooped off at us with everything she'd got. She'd only been supposed to have eight anti-aircraft guns, but fire was coming from more than eight places – in fact she looked just one big flash. The explosions threw the flying boat about and we could hear bits of shrapnel hit the hull. Luckily only a few penetrated.

The Catalina was able to report the ship's position and another Catalina took over the shadow duties. Eventually the *Bismarck* was put out of useful service by Fleet Air Arm Swordfish torpedo bombers. It was also

Blue Angels at Sea and Sky Spectacular in Jacksonville Beach, USA, in October 2015. (US Navy Mass Communication Specialist 3rd Class, Timothy Schumaker)

attacked by Royal Navy ships and then was scuttled by its own crew. It sank on 27 May 1941.

BLUE ANGELS

The US Navy's *Blue Angels* (officially the US Navy Flight Demonstration Squadron) are renowned for their close formation flying, with some of the manoeuvres being flown with wingtips only a few feet apart. The team, whose name stems from a New York nightclub known by one of the original members, fly with US Navy and US Marine pilots.

Since their inception in 1946 they have flown the following aircraft:[7]

Aircraft Flown	Dates
Grumman F6F Hellcat	1946
Grumman F8F-1 Bearcat	1946–1949
Grumman F9F-2 Panther (During the Korean War the team saw action as VF-191 Satan's Kittens squadron)	1949–1950
Grumman F9F-5 Panther (Chance-Vought F7U-1 Cutlass were flown in part of the 1953 season)	1951–1955
Grumman F9F-8 Cougar	1955–1957
Grumman F11F-1 Tiger	1957–1968
McDonnell Douglas F-4J Phantom	1969–1974
McDonnell Douglas A-4F Skyhawk	1974–1987
McDonnell Douglas F/A-18 Hornet	1987–present

BOEING 7-7 SERIES

Britain had built the world's first jet airliner with the Comet but was unable to maintain this lead in commercial jet travel. American manufacturer Boeing soon gained the upper hand with its 707 aircraft. This was the first in a series of successful types.[8]

Aircraft Type	Engines	First flight	Number built	Notes
707	4	15 July 1954	1,010	A customised 707 known as SAM 26000 served as *Air Force One* and brought President John F. Kennedy's body back from Dallas in 1963.

Qantas Boeing 707 N707JT owned by John Travolta. (Phinalanji via Flickr Creative Commons 2.0)

717	4	31 August 1956	803	A military aircraft, known as the KC-135 Stratotanker. Number reassigned to MD-95 after merger of Boeing and McDonnell Douglas in the 1990s.
727	3	9 February 1963	1,832	First three-engined jet airliner.
737	2	9 April 1967	8,800+	Highest-selling commercial jetliner.
747	4	9 February 1969	1,500+	The 'Jumbo Jet' was the world's first wide-body airliner.
757	2	19 February 1982	1,050	The final 757 was delivered to Singapore Airlines in 2005.
767	2	26 September 1981	1,000+	The first twin-engined airliner to receive regulatory approval for extended overseas flights.
777	2	12 June 1994	1,400+	Pandas delivered to Edinburgh Zoo in 2011 were flown from China in a cargo version of the 777.
787 Dream-liner	2	15 December 2009	360+	Reported to be 20 per cent more fuel efficient than its predecessor.

C IS FOR...

CELEBRITY PILOTS

With money and time available to pursue their interest, many celebrities have been able to enjoy the expensive hobby of flying:

| Tom Cruise | Actor |
| Gary Numan | Musician |

Dave Gilmour	Musician
Bruce Dickinson	Musician/airline pilot
John Travolta	Actor
Harrison Ford	Actor
Cliff Robertson	Actor
Dave Rowntree	Musician
James May	TV presenter
Carol Vorderman	TV presenter

CENTURY SERIES

The American military numerical designation system for fighter aircraft reached 100 in the 1950s and this led to a range of supersonic fighters known as the Century Series:

Convair F-102 Delta Dagger

With its first flight in 1953, the Convair F-102 was the world's first supersonic fighter able to operate in all weathers. This delta-winged machine saw service mainly in the United States Air Force as its primary air defence fighter. It carried its weapons internally, the first aircraft to have this arrangement. A thousand were built.

Convair F-106 Delta Dart

The F-106 first flew in 1956. It was designed to be the chief all-weather air defence fighter for the US Air Force. Delta Darts were armed with the Genie air-to-air nuclear missile, intended to be fired at large formations of enemy bombers. The Delta Dart was capable of going more than twice the speed of sound. It was retired from active combat-ready duty in 1988 and was used as target drone until 1997.[9]

Lockheed F-104 Starfighter

The F-104's first flight was in 1954. Described as 'a missile with a man in it' the Mach 2-capable fighter had a long streamlined fuselage with very thin and very short wings: they measured only 7½ft from the fuselage to the wing tip. The Starfighter was exported to several countries including Japan, Italy, Norway, Belgium, Holland and Germany. The latter experienced a high casualty rate caused by the Luftwaffe's inexperience of handling such a high-tech aircraft.

McDonnell F-101 Voodoo

The F-101's first flight was in 1954. The twin-engined fighter was initially envisaged as being a bomber escort but this was abandoned and it was developed as a fighter-bomber and then for the reconnaissance role. Voodoos brought back vital photoreconnaissance information during the 1962 Cuban Missile Crisis.

North American F-100 Super Sabre

The F-100 was America's first supersonic fighter with its first flight in 1953. Showing its capability, the Super Sabre went supersonic on its first flight, despite flying with an inferior engine to that fitted to production models. It was used extensively in US Air Force service, flying missions in Vietnam where a F-100 made the first USAF kill when a North Vietnamese MiG-17 was shot down on 4 April 1965. F-100s also served with overseas operators. Over 2,200 were built.

Republic F-105 Thunderchief

The F-105 first flew in 1955. It was the largest single-engine combat aircraft ever built, and was only 10ft short of the length of a Second World War B-17 Flying Fortress. The F-105, known as *The Thud* by its crews, was intended to be primarily a nuclear bomber but was used in Vietnam as a conventional bomber and an electronic-warfare platform. Over 800 were built. Almost half of all the F-105s built were lost in the Vietnam War.

CIVIL AIRCRAFT REGISTRATION PREFIXES

Civilian aircraft are all officially registered. Each aircraft, has its individual registration numbers (or letters) along with a country code. The International Civil Aviation Organization supervises the system. The country codes include the following:

A7	Qatar	EW	Belarus	JA	Japan
B	China	F	France	LV	Argentina
C	Canada	G	United	M	Isle of Man
CU	Cuba		Kingdom	N	USA
D	Germany	HB	Switzerland	OE	Austria
EC	Spain	I	Italy	OH	Finland

OK	Czech		Korea	VT	India
	Republic	RA	Russia	XA/XB/XC	Mexico
OO	Belgium	TT	Chad	YI	Iraq
P	North	VH	Australia	Z	Zimbabwe

COLOUR SCHEMES

As airliners are predominantly painted white they offer a great opportunity for being adorned with special schemes.

Airline	Aircraft	Serial	Details	Year first flown
Air New Zealand	Boeing 777	ZK-OKP	Characters from film *The Hobbit: An Unexpected Journey.*	2012
British Airways	Airbus A319	G-DBCB G-DBCD G-EUPA G-EUPD G-EUPG G-EUPH G-EUOH	Golden dove design to celebrate London Olympic Games 2012.	2012
British Airways	Airbus A319	G-EUPC	Firefly design. Aircraft used to carry Olympic flame to London Olympic Games 2012.	2012
Air New Zealand	Boeing 777	ZK-OKO	177ft-long dragon to mark film *The Hobbit: The Desolation of Smaug.*	2013
WestJet	Boeing 737	C-GWSZ	Mickey Mouse as Sorcerer Mickey.	2013
ANA (All Nippon Airways)	Boeing 767	JA604A	R2-D2 and new robot BB-8 to mark release of film *Star Wars: The Force Awakens.*	2015
ANA (All Nippon Airways)	Boeing 787	JA873A	R2-D2 to mark release of film *Star Wars: The Force Awakens.*	2015
WestJet	Boeing 737	C-GWSV	Characters from the Disney film *Frozen.*	2015
ANA (All Nippon Airways)	Boeing 777	JA789A	New robot BB-8 to mark release of film *Star Wars: The Force Awakens.*	2016

D IS FOR...

DEATH DIP

Lincoln Beachey was the first stunt pilot in America. He began by flying dirigibles, before deciding heavier-than-air machines were the future. He learnt to fly with Glenn Curtiss and began a career of daredevil exhibition flights in front of astonished crowds.

He was first to perfect a recovery from a spin and after carrying out the first loop in America became adept in repeating the manoeuvre over and over. His thirst for exciting flights saw him become the first to fly over Niagara Falls in 1911. He dived down through the mists and flew under the Falls View Honeymoon Bridge.

He teamed up with car driver Barney Oldfield and among the stunts performed was one where Beachey would fly so low he could knock off Oldfield's hat.

Perhaps the most outrageous of his stunts was blowing up the battleship USS *Oregon* – or at least a model of it – a fact not known to the 80,000 onlookers who were shocked at this demonstration of aerial bombing.

Among Beachey's repertoire was the 'death dip' where he would dive straight down towards the ground then pull up with only feet remaining. Orville Wright said of Beachey: 'He's the most wonderful flyer I ever saw. He's the greatest aviator of them all.'

In the book *The Genius of Aviation,* Beachey wrote:

> The Silent Reaper of Souls and I shook hands that day. Thousands of times we have engaged in a race among the clouds – plunging headlong in breathless flight – diving and circling with awful speed through ethereal space. And, many times, when the dazzling sunlight has blinded my eyes and sudden darkness has numbed all my senses, I have imagined him close at my heels. On such occasions I have defied him, but in so doing have experienced fright which I cannot explain. Today the old fellow and I are pals.

In 1915 the 'Silent Reaper' gained the final upper hand, as the wings of Beachey's machine collapsed while demonstrating over San Francisco Bay. He was found still strapped into his seat.[10]

Lincoln Beachey photographed in 1912. (Library of Congress, Prints & Photographs Division, LC-USZ62-17970)

DEFUNCT AIRLINES OF BRITAIN

Britain has seen many airlines. In the competitive market of commercial aviation many have become defunct through merger or financial hardship. The list of those airlines no longer flying includes these twenty:[11]

Airline	Ceased Operations
Air UK	1998
Autair International Airways	1970
BKS Air Transport	1970
British Air Ferries	1979
British Caledonian	1988
British Eagle International Airlines	1968
British European Airways	1974
British Midland International	2012
British Overseas Airways Corporation	1974
British United Airways	1970
British World Airlines	2001
Cambrian Airways	1974
Channel Airways	1972
Court Line Aviation	1974
Dan-Air	1992
Hunting-Clan Air Transport	1960
Imperial Airways	1939
Invicta International Airlines Ltd	1982
Northeast Airlines	1976
Silver City Airlines	1963

DESERT ISLAND DISCS

Among the guests that have appeared on the long-running BBC Radio programme *Desert Island Discs*, few have been recipients of the Victoria Cross. One guest who did recieve a Victoria Cross appeared on 19 February 1944: Wing Commander Guy Gibson. The format of the show requires the guest to select music that they would listen to while marooned on their hypothetical desert island. Gibson's choices were:

Warsaw Concerto (from wartime film *Dangerous Moonlight*) – London
      Symphony Orchestra
Where or When (from musical *Babes in Arms*) – Jack Hylton and his Orchestra
A Thousand and One Nights Waltz – Symphony Orchestra
The Flying Dutchman – Berlin State Opera Orchestra
'If I Had My Way' – Bing Crosby
The Marines Hymn – Fred Waring & His Pennsylvanians
Royal Air Force March Past – The Central Band of the RAF
Ride of the Valkyries – Queen's Hall Light Orchestra

Gibson said of the last tune: 'It reminds me of a bombing raid. Though I don't say it's like one'.

He returned to flying operations and was killed over the Netherlands in September 1944.[12]

DISPLAY SCHEDULE

The RAF have a long history of organising 'At Home' airshows to allow the public the opportunity to see their air force and its aircraft at close hand. One of the most popular shows was at RAF Leuchars in Fife, which held its airshow around the middle of September to mark the Battle of Britain. Showing the breadth of aircraft operated by the RAF at the time. The show in 1973 had the following line-up of flying participants included in the Programme of Events:

1300	*Chipmunk/Glider Aerobatics*
1316	*Chipmunk display (East Lothian Air Squadron)*
1400	*Hunter solo aerobatics*
1408	*VC10 display*
1413	*Lightning/Phantom flypast*
1414	*Lightning formation display*
1420	*Phantom formation display*

1429   Phantom
1439   Whirlwind display
1452   Dominie display
1458   Argosy - Blue Knights para drop
1509   Sea King display
1515   Vulcan display
1523   Victor display
1529   F-104 solo aerobatics (Royal Netherlands Air Force)
1539   Hercules display
1545   Nimrod display
1552   Canberra overfly
1552   Buccaneer display
1559   Harrier display
1610   F-111 flypast
1612   Chipmunk solo aerobatics (East Lothian Air Squadron)
1616   F-111 flypast
1618   Magister aerobatics (Les Diables Rouge, Belgian Air Force)
1628   Gnat display
1635   Spitfire display
1642   Gannet display
1649   Hunter display
1657   Belfast display
1704   Shackleton display
1710   Phantom solo aerobatics

The RAF Leuchars Pipe Band will perform the ceremony of Beating the Retreat.

Forty years after this dispaly the final airshow was held as the airbase became home to British Army units.

DONCASTER v BLACKPOOL

In 1909 a spat broke out between two English towns over which was going to be the first to host the UK's inaugural aviation meeting. The organisers of the Blackpool Aviation Week had become annoyed when they heard that Doncaster had made plans to hold their own event – and starting three days before theirs.

The intervention of the Aero Club of Great Britain (who supported the Blackpool event) was not enough to prevent Doncaster holding their event between 15 and 23 October, where the first man to pilot a powered aircraft in the United Kingdom – Samuel F. Cody – flew. At Blackpool aviation pioneers Hubert Latham and Henry Farman took part, with Farman winning the largest amount in prize money: £2,400. Both events lost money despite 200,000 spectators attending at Blackpool and a claimed one million going to Doncaster.

DOWNWIND

On 10 February 1938, 111 Squadron commander Squadron Leader John Gillan flew a Hawker Hurricane from RAF Turnhouse outside Edinburgh, to Northolt in London. His flight took 48 minutes, covering 327 miles at an average speed of 408.75mph. His speed was achieved by a helpful tailwind and earned him the nickname 'Downwind' Gillan.

E IS FOR...

EARLY AVIATION PIONEERS WHO DIED IN FLYING ACCIDENTS

Flying in the early days of aviation was particularly dangerous. There were no manuals for these machines that were also constantly being adapted as they went along. Basic principles of aeronautical engineering were learnt through trial and error and deaths were commonplace. These are some of the pioneers who died in non-military accidents, before the Second World War.

Aviator	Country of Origin	Year of Death
Otto Lilienthal	Germany	1896
Salomon August Andrée	Sweden	1897
Percy Pilcher	UK	1899
Thomas E. Selfridge	USA	1908
Eugène Lefebvre	France	1909
Ferdinand Ferber	France	1909
Archibald Hoxsey	USA	1910
Cecil Grace	Chile	1910

Charles Rolls	UK	1910
John Moisant	USA	1910
Jorge Chávez	Peru	1910
Léon Delagrange	France	1910
Ralph Johnstone	USA	1910
Édouard Nieuport	France	1911
Eugene Ely	USA	1911
Paul Engelhard	Germany	1911
W. Alfred Pietschker	Germany	1911
D. Leslie Allen	Ireland	1912
Calbraith Perry Rodgers	USA	1912
Julia Clark	USA	1912
Harriet Quimby	USA	1912
Samuel F. Cody	USA	1913
Gustav Hamel	UK	1914
Henry Post	USA	1914

Eugène Lefebvre in Wright biplane at Reims in 1909. (Library of Congress, Prints & Photographs Division, LC-USZ62-48804)

Gaston Caudron	France	1915
Lincoln J. Beachey	USA	1915
John Alcock	UK	1919
Jules Védrines	France	1919
Raymonde Baroness de Laroche (aka Élisa Leontine Deroche)	France	1919
Ormer Locklear	USA	1920
Harry Hawker	Australia	1921
Ross Smith	Australia	1922
Lawrence Sperry	UK	1923
Bessie Coleman	USA	1926
Charles Nungesser	France	1927
Roald Amundsen	Norway	1928
Comte Henry de La Vaulx	France	1930
George Herbert Scott	UK	1930
Ruth Alexander	USA	1930
Edward Heath	USA	1931
Eddie Stinson	USA	1932
Bert Hinkler	Australia	1933
Charles Ulm	Australia	1934
Charles Kingsford Smith	Australia	1935
Wiley Post	USA	1935
Juan de la Cierva	Spain	1936
Tom Campbell Black	UK	1936
Amelia Earhart	USA	1937
Francisco Sarabia	Mexico	1939

EAST FORTUNE

Scotland's main aviation museum is the National Museum of Flight in East Lothian. The airfield at East Fortune was formerly a Royal Naval Air Service base (the R34 airship began its famous double-Atlantic crossing flights from it in 1919) and during the Second World War it hosted RAF Training Command and then Coastal Command aircraft. The museum opened in 1975 and its collection contains some iconic aircraft:

Armstrong Whitworth Meteor
   NF.14
Avro Anson
Avro Vulcan B.2A
BAC 111
BAC/Aérospatiale Concorde
Beagle Auster A.61 Terrier 1
Beagle Bulldog
Beech E.18.S
Blackburn Buccaneer S.2B
Bristol Beaufighter TF.X
Bristol Bolingbroke IVT
British Aerospace Dragonfly 2
British Aerospace Jetstream
Britten-Norman Islander
de Havilland Comet 4C
de Havilland Dove
de Havilland Dragon
de Havilland Puss Moth
de Havilland Sea Venom FAW.22
de Havilland Tiger Moth
Druine Turbulent G-AVPC

English Electric Lightning F.2A
General Aircraft Cygnet
Hawker Sea Hawk F.2
Hawker Siddeley Harrier DB.3
Kay Type 33/1 gyroplane
McDonnell Douglas F-4S Phantom
Messerschmitt Me 163B Komet
Miles M.18 Mk II
Morane Saulnier MS 505a Criquet
Panavia Tornado F3
Percival Provost
Pilcher Hawk
Piper Comanche 260B
Piper PA-38 Tomahawk
Saunders-Roe Skeeter AOP.12
Scottish Aviation Bulldog
Scottish Aviation Twin Pioneer
SEPECAT Jaguar GR1A
Vickers Supermarine Spitfire
   LF.XVIe
Vickers Viscount
Weir W-2 autogyro

'EIGHT MILES HIGH'

Despite being tagged as a drug song, 'Eight Miles High' by American 1960s pop group The Byrds is partly a planespotting song. When interviewed on Radio Scotland's *Banned History of Rock and Roll* in 2007, singer Roger McGuinn said that as a group they would go down and watch the planes landing at their nearest airport.

In 1965, they had come up with a particular tune and were looking for a title. McGuinn was asked how high airliners flew and said about 36,000ft – or 6 miles. The writer of the song, David Crosby, thought this didn't sound right, and so, as the Beatles had released a single called 'Eight Days a Week', he thought that number sounded cool, so 'Eight Miles High' it became.

£87,500

The cost of a pilot's training course at CAE Oxford Aviation Academy in 2015 was £87,500. Further fees upwards of £20,000 would be required to be trained on a specific type of airliner.[13]

ENGINES

British engine manufacturers Bristol and Rolls-Royce used different sources of inspiration in naming their engines.

Bristol Engines Given Names From Greek and Roman Mythology

Aquila	Neptune	Perseus
Centaurus	Proteus	Phoenix
Hercules	Olympus	Taurus
Hydra	Orpheus	Theseus
Jupiter	Orion	Titan
Mercury	Pegasus	

Rolls-Royce Engines Named After British Rivers

Avon	Exe	Trent
Clyde	Nene	Tweed
Conway	Soar	Tyne
Dart	Spey	
Derwent	Tay	

Rolls-Royce Engines Named After Birds of Prey

Buzzard	Goshawk	Merlin
Condor	Griffon	Peregrine
Eagle	Hawk	Vulture
Falcon	Kestrel	

ERIC 'WINKLE' BROWN

Often described as Britain's most accomplished pilot, Captain Eric Brown's life and career seems fictional, but all of it is true.

- Attended the 1936 Berlin Olympics.
- Flew with First World War German ace Ernst Udet.
- Was arrested by the SS at the outbreak of war.
- Shot down two German Focke-Wulf Condor patrol aircraft.
- Survived a torpedo attack on the aircraft carrier HMS *Audacious*.
- First man to land a twin-engined aircraft on an aircraft carrier (Mosquito).
- First man to land a jet on an aircraft carrier (Vampire).
- Performed most ever aircraft carrier landings (2,407).
- Flew the most number of aircraft of any pilot (487).
- Crashed a Fairey Firefly onto the deck of an aircraft carrier during testing.
- Had his home hit by a V-1 Doodlebug.
- Took the surrender of a German-held airfield in Denmark in 1945 after landing, thinking it already secured.
- Flew captured German aircraft, including Arado Ar 234 and Messerschmitt Me 163 Komet.
- Interrogated Bergen-Belsen concentration camp commander Josef Kramer and female supervisor Irma Grese.
- Interviewed Hermann Goering before the Nuremberg trials.
- Survived a serious crash testing a new jet fighter flying boat (Saunders-Roe SR.1/A).
- Was commander of Royal Naval Air Station *Lossiemouth* for three years.

Brown put his longevity in a dangerous occupation partly down to his height (which gave him his nickname). Being smaller meant he was less likely to lose his legs in a crash or, in the case of the de Havilland DH.108, have his neck broken by the violent oscillations that had killed Geoffrey de Havilland. Another factor was his careful pre-flight procedures. In 2013 Brown said: 'I was always meticulous in my preparation.' He died in 2016, aged 97.

EVEREST

One of the most memorable flights in the 'Golden Age' of aviation was the attempt to fly over Mount Everest for the first time. Two Westland

Wallace biplanes were prepared, and for such appropriately named aircraft, both flown by Scotsmen: David McIntyre and Douglas Douglas-Hamilton, Marquis of Clydesdale. The event attracted much publicity and the headlines in *The Scotsman* newspaper tell the story of the epic flight:

- 'Over Mt Everest: Lord Clydesdale to Pilot Aeroplane' (20 September 1932)
- 'Flight Over Everest: Successful Test of Aeroplanes' (25 January 1933)
- 'Everest Expedition: Fliers Leave for India' (17 February 1933)
- 'An Everest Plane: Pilot Satisfied with Test Flight in India' (16 March 1933)
- 'Everest Test Flight In India: British Airmen Reach Altitude of 37,000 Feet' (17 March 1933)
- 'Party Leaves Karachi for Base in Bihar' (21 March 1933)
- 'Two Planes to Attempt to Reach Altitude of 35,000 Feet' (25 March 1933)
- '73mph Wind: Delays Test Flight Over Everest' (28 March 1933)
- 'Everest Conquered' (4 April 1933)

F IS FOR...

FAIREY LONG-RANGE MONOPLANE

This aircraft exactly reflected its name. It was designed specifically for long duration flights with its wingspan of 82ft giving it a large amount of lift. Two notable flights were made with the type:

Distance (miles)	Duration	Dates	Aircraft	Notes
4,130	50 hours, 37 minutes	24–26 April 1929	J9479	First non-stop flight from UK to India
5,309	57 hours, 25 minutes	6–8 February 1933	K1991	First non-stop flight from UK to South Africa

Although J9479's flight to India was a British record, it didn't attain the world record and so another world record attempt was made, this time to South Africa. This flight in December 1929 saw the aircraft crash in Tunisia and both crew members killed. A second monoplane was built and K1991 achieved the distance record in 1933.[14]

FAITH, HOPE AND CHARITY

The island of Malta was strategically important for the Allies in the Second World War as it afforded a base to attack the German and Italian forces in the Mediterranean and North Africa. The day after Italy joined the war on 10 June 1940 its aircraft began bombing the island, beginning a campaign that would last several years. The island was subjected to heavy aerial bombardment, and at one point was bombed consecutively for 154 days. In April 1942 the George Cross was awarded to 'honour her brave people'.

Initially the island's aerial defenders were a handful of Sea Gladiator biplanes – three of which were later given the names *Faith*, *Hope* and *Charity* by the Maltese press – although they had been joined by four Hurricanes flown out from the UK in June.

Other aircraft were flown out from land bases but most of the fighter reinforcements were to be transported by aircraft carrier and then flown onto the island. In total, 333 Hurricanes and 367 Spitfires were successfully delivered to shore up the defences. Fears of an Axis invasion receded with the success of the Allied campaign in North Africa in 1943.

FASTER THAN THE SUN

The Fairey Delta 2 (FD.2) was the first aircraft to fly faster than 1,000mph in level flight. Never intended to be a production fighter, the sleek craft was solely a high-speed research vehicle. The delta-winged jet was powered by only one engine, a Rolls-Royce Avon, which in reheat could produce around 10,000lb of thrust.

When it created a new world record on 10 March 1956, the FD.2 broke the previous one, held by the United States' Horace Hanes in a North American F-100C Super Sabre, by over 300mph. In order to satisfy the criteria of a world record run, Twiss had to fly two legs, in opposing directions. He reached 1,117mph on the first and 1,147mph on the second – making his average speed 1,132mph. As the speed of the Earth's rotation is 1,000mph, Twiss was flying faster than the sun – the phrase became the title of his memoir.

F-15 on its
first flight in
1972. (USAF)

Twiss had flown with the navy in the Second World War before becoming chief test pilot at Fairey. When the company was sold he joined Fairey Marine which led to him appearing in the James Bond film *From Russia With Love* where he steered one of the powerboats chasing 007.

FIDO (FOG, INTENSE DISPERSAL OF)

FIDO was a Second World War British system of illuminating runways by burning petrol from burners that ran up both sides of the runway. FIDO is claimed to have saved the lives of up to 10,000 bomber crews returning to base during foggy conditions.

FILMS WITH SPECTACULAR PLANE CRASHES

1. *Alive* (1993)
2. *Cast Away* (2000)
3. *Con Air* (1997)
4. *Fearless* (1993)
5. *Final Destination* (2000)
6. *Flight* (2012)
7. *Flight of the Phoenix* (2004)
8. *Knowing* (2009)
9. *The Grey* (2010)
10. *World War Z* (2014)

FIRE STARTER

Aircraft set on fire by lighter

A 16-year-old boy who, while trying to fill a cigarette lighter, caused a Mosquito aircraft to catch fire and suffer damage estimated at £2,000, pleaded 'Guilty' at Hatfield Juvenile Court yesterday to 'causing a conflagration in a protected place'. The charge was dismissed under the Probation of Offenders Act, the Chairman stating that the boy had committed the offence accidentally and had received a lesson which he would remember all his life.

A police sergeant said the boy, who was employed by the de Havilland Company on aircraft maintenance, took his father's cigarette lighter to work to repair it. While working in a hangar he got under a Mosquito aircraft and was trying to fill the lighter by holding it under a leaking petrol pipe when he accidentally ignited it. His hands were burned, and he dropped the lighter close to the Mosquito, which caught fire.

The Times, 6 July 1943

FIRST FLIGHT

James Tytler, chemist in Edinburgh, has been for some time past employed in the construction of a fire-balloon. Its dimensions are about 40ft in height, and 30ft in diameter. It was the intention of the projector to have ascended with his balloon about the beginning of this month, during the race week, but things not being in that forwardness and perfection he expected, he was obliged to postpone his aerial journey. On the morning of the 27th however he made a decisive experiment. About five o'clock the balloon was inflated and soon manifested a disposition to ascend. Mr Tytler took his seat and with inexpressible satisfaction felt himself raised with great power from the earth. The machine entangled itself among the branches of a tree and by a rope belonging to the mast, which raised it, so that its power of ascension was greatly weakened. However, when the obstacles were removed, it flew up to the height of 350ft, as measured by a line left hanging from the bottom of the basket. The morning was calm, and therefore the balloon went but a small way, as no furnace was taken up with it. It soon returned to the earth, without any damage to the projector who, in testimony of his security, returned, while in the air, the huzzas of the spectators, and on his return was overwhelmed with their congratulations.

The Scots Magazine, August 1784

The 'projector' was James Tytler, the first person to fly in the United Kingdom. This first aeronaut was a Scot, the son of a church minister from Fern, near Brechin, Angus – born the same year as Bonnie Prince Charlie began his doomed Jacobite rebellion.

Tytler studied medicine at the University of Edinburgh and worked as a ship's surgeon and then a pharmacist. Always running into debt, he found his vocation as an editor, and in 1759 he started work on the Second Edition of the *Encyclopaedia Britannica*. It was during this research that he read about the Montgolfier Brothers' early experiments in ballooning in France, which inspired his interest.

Through the eighteenth-century version of crowdfunding – public subscription – he raised enough money to build his hot-air balloon and on 27 August 1784 it carried him from near Holyrood Palace in Edinburgh to Restalrig, a flight of around half a mile.

Despite Tytler's success, the Italian balloonist Vincent Lunardi quickly overshadowed him. In these days of revolution, Tytler fell foul of the government after publishing a radical pamphlet and quickly exiled himself to America, where he died in 1804.[15]

FIRST OF THE KIND

An aircraft's first flight is a critical moment. In the modern era with more sophisticated design methods much less is left to chance and aircraft are expected to perform exactly to specification. Earlier first flights were more anxious. Ten first flights of some famous aircraft were:[16]

Serial	Type	Date	Location	Pilot	Pilot's Comments
K5083	Hawker Hurricane	6 November 1935	Brooklands, Surrey	George Bulman	'A piece of cake.'
NX14988	Douglas DC-3	17 December 1935	Clover Field, Santa Monica, CA, USA	Carl A. Cover	'Rather routine' (Flight engineer Frank Collbohm)
K5054	Spitfire	5 March 1936	Eastleigh, Hampshire	Joseph 'Mutt' Summers	'I don't want anything touched.'
BT308	Avro Lancaster	9 January 1941	Ringway, Manchester	Sam Brown	'It was marvellous. Easy to handle and light on the controls.'

G-ALVG	de Havilland Comet	27 July 1949	Hatfield, Hertfordshire	John Cunningham	'Very promising. Very quick.'
Bu. No. 142259	McDonnell Douglas F-4 Phantom II (F-4H-1)	27 May 1958	Lambert Field, St Louis, MO, USA	Bob Little	Unrecorded
N7470 'City of Everett'	Boeing 747	9 February 1969	Paine Field, Everett, WA, USA	Jack Wadell	'The plane is ridiculously easy to fly. It almost lands itself.'
F-WTSS	Concorde	2 March 1969	Toulouse, France	André Turcat	'Finally the big bird flies, and I can say now that it flies pretty well.'
71-0280	McDonnell Douglas F-15 Eagle	27 July 1972	Edwards AFB, CA, USA	Irving L. Burrows	'It was just like the simulator!'
72-01567	General Dynamics F-16	20 January 1974	Edwards AFB, CA, USA	Phil F. Oestricher	Unrecorded

$5

The ticket price for a passenger on the world's first commercial flight was $5. The route was between the Floridian cities of St Petersburg and Tampa and passengers were carried one at a time. The service, which began in January 1914, took 23 minutes for each journey.[17]

5,095

Number of F-4 Phantoms built. The vast majority were constructed in America, with 127 being built in Japan by Mitsubishi. The multi-role Phantom first flew in 1958 and versions are still in service to the present day.

FLEET AIR ARM

The Royal Naval Air Service dated back to the First World War until it was merged with the Royal Flying Corps into the newly formed Royal Air Force in 1918. Navy aviators were never comfortable with this arrangement and twenty years later just before the start of the Second World War, the Fleet Air Arm was formed. Its most famous exploit of the war was the attack on the Italian port of Taranto by torpedo-carrying Fairey Swordfish biplanes.

Post-war the Fleet Air Arm saw action in the Korean War and by January 1960 it was flying a mixture of helicopters, propeller airborne early warning (AEW) aircraft and fighter and ground attack jets. The Royal Navy had six carriers to which the following aircraft were assigned.[18]

Ship	Aircraft	Squadron
HMS *Ark Royal*	Scimitar F.1	800
	Scimitar F.1	807
	Whirlwind HAS.7	820
	Whirlwind HAS.7	824
	Sea Vixen FAW.1	892
HMS *Centaur*	Sea Hawk FGA.6	801
	Gannet AS.4	810
	Skyraider AEW.1	849 'D' flight
HMS *Victorious*	Scimitar F.1	803
	Gannet ECM.6	831 'A' flight
	Sea Venom 21	831 'B' flight
	Gannet AEW.3	849 'B' flight
	Sea Venom FAW.22	893
HMS *Eagle*	Sea Hawk FGA.6	806
HMS *Albion*	Whirlwind HAS.7	815
	Gannet AEW.3	849 'C' flight
	Sea Venom FAW.22	894
HMS *Bulwark*	Whirlwind HAS.7	848

FLYING BOATS

The world's last regular flying boat route was that flown by Australian operator Ansett Flying Boat Services. It operated two Short S.25 Sandringhams from Sydney to Lord Howe Island, 420 miles out in the Pacific.

The four-engined Sandringhams had started life in the Second World War as Sunderlands before being converted to civilian use. Ansett ended the service in 1974 when an airport opened on the island.

Both Sandringhams were preserved with one – VH-BRF *Islander* – on show in Florida at Kermit Weeks' Fantasy of Flight museum and the other – VH-BRC *Beachcomber* – on display in Southampton's Solent Sky museum.

FLYING FLEA

The Flying Flea
How to Build and Fly It!

Complete instructions and detailed drawings for building this famous French light plane. Authentic translation from the French of Henri Mignet, the designer. Profusely illustrated and absorbing book recommended to everyone interested in aviation. Price $3.00 post-paid. Imported from England.
Popular Aviation, 608 S Dearborn St, Chicago IL.

Advert in *Popular Aviation* magazine, February 1937

The Flying Flea was a French home-built aircraft that first flew in 1933. It was advertised as being able to be built and flown by anyone but several crashes severely dented enthusiasm for it.

FOO FIGHTERS

Fireball Mystery
American Fliers Puzzled by New Nazi 'Secret Weapon'

American fighter pilots engaged in flying night intruder missions over Germany report the Nazis have come up with a new 'secret weapon' – mysterious 'balls of fire' which race along beside their planes for miles like will o' the wisps.

Tank pilots have dubbed them 'foo fighters' and at first thought they might explode, but so far there is no indication that any planes have been damaged by them.

Some pilots have expressed belief that the 'foo fighter' was designed strictly as a psychological weapon. Intelligence reports seem to indicate it is radio-controlled from the ground and can keep pace with planes flying 300 miles per hour.

Lt Donald Melers of Chicago, Illinois, said there are three types of 'foo fighters': red balls of fire that fly along at wing tip, a vertical row of three balls of fire which fly in front of the planes, and a group of about 15 lights which follow the plane at a distance, flickering on and off.

This report from the *Lawrence, Kansas Daily Journal-World*, on 2 January 1945, highlighted a phenomenon that was treated seriously by Allied pilots. Quite what these balls of light and fire were has never been fully explained and their appearance has been included in the catalogue of possible extra-terrestrial UFO sightings.

FORMATION FLYING

The leader of the formation flies a streamer on each side and one from his rudder. The deputy leader has the two side streamers only. Others in the formation may fly just one streamer to show they are leading a flight of three.

The leader can talk to all the pilots by wireless telephone. He has also some simple manoeuvres, which he can do. A roll from side to side is a signal to 'Close Up' the formation; a dip, a rise and a dip means 'Open Out'. If a roll is made to the left and then back to the horizontal it means 'Change Direction'. A small drop in height is a signal for 'Prepare to Dive'. A quick rise means 'About Turn'. In wartime a violent roll from side to side means 'Enemy in Sight'.

From 1933's *The Book About Aircraft*

486 SQUADRON PILOTS

In the spring of 1943 Squadron Leader Desmond Scott was given command of 486 Squadron, then flying Hawker Typhoons. In his book *Typhoon Pilot* he describes the experience of being in a unit faced with attacking German-occupied France before the Normandy landings and attempting to intercept Luftwaffe raiders.

In time-honoured fashion, some of his pilots were known by their nicknames:[19]

Nickname	Name	Details
'Bluey'	Rober J. Dall	Died 4 July 1945 performing aerobatics before leaving squadron for a posting to Burma.
'Happy'	L.J. Appleton	Hit by friendly fire on 13 January 1945 and crashed. Repatriated to New Zealand.

RAF Typhoon at Prestwick Airport in September 2015. (Norman Ferguson)

'Hyphen'	Keith G. Taylor-Cannon	Killed in action 13 April 1945.
'Spike'	Arthur E. Umbers	Killed in action 14 February 1945.
'Woe'	James G. Wilson	Shot down in 1945 and seriously injured but recovered. Died in 1998.

G IS FOR...

G-NA

In the Battle of Britain, Flight Lieutenant James Nicolson won Fighter Command's only Victoria Cross of the war for his attempt to shoot down a German Messerschmitt Me 110 while his Hawker Hurricane was in flames. Nicolson was about to bail out but had stayed in the burning aircraft to keep firing. He bailed out but was badly burnt. To add insult to injury, Home Guard members shot him at as he descended under his parachute. Nicolson returned to front-line operations, only to die in 1945.

In 2015, to mark the 75th anniversary of the Battle of Britain, ZK349, one of the RAF's current front-line Eurofighter Typhoon fighters, was painted in a special colour scheme to reflect that of Nicolson's aircraft. The codes G-NA were applied along with the green and brown camouflage pattern used at that time. The Typhoon was a popular sight on the airshow scene in 2015.

GILMORE

Gilmore was a regular passenger in aircraft flown by American pilot Roscoe Turner in the 1930s. He was unusual in that he was a four-legged animal – a lion. Turner had arranged a sponsorship arrangement with the Gilmore Oil Company and as their Red Lion products featured a lion, he thought up the publicity idea involving a real, live king of the jungle.

Turner flew as a barnstormer and airline pilot and also won several air races before setting up a training centre for aircrew during the Second World War. When Gilmore died he was stuffed and is now part of the Smithsonian National Air and Space Museum's collection. When he died, Turner was buried in Crown Hill Cemetery, Indianapolis.

GORDON BENNETT

The origins of the exclamatory phrase are not defined for certain but there are reasons to believe it comes from one man: James Gordon Bennett Jnr, known as Gordon Bennett to differentiate from his wealthy father, a Scottish émigré who became rich after founding the *New York Herald* in 1835. When his father died Bennett took over the running of the paper. (It was Bennett who sent Henry Stanley to find Scottish missionary David Livingstone in Africa.)

Gordon Bennett's inheritance of his father's fortune ensured the funding of a playboy lifestyle and he put money into sponsoring competitions, in automobile racing, ballooning and air racing – the first of which was held at the first international airshow at Reims in 1909.

The use of his name to reflect surprise is believed to come, in part, from an incident at the home of his future in-laws where Bennett was so intoxicated he mistook a fireplace for the lavatory – in front of guests. His engagement was broken off after this scandal and Bennett moved to Europe.[20]

GRUMMAN'S CATS

American manufacturer Grumman built aircraft for the US Navy and during the Second World War its fighter aircraft were named after cats, beginning a tradition that lasted until its final fighter jet: the Tomcat.[21]

Aircraft	First Flight	Notes
F4F Wildcat	September 1937	Almost 8,000 were built. Flown by the Royal Navy as the Martlet. A seaplane version – the Wildcatfish – was developed but only one was made.
F6F Hellcat	June 1942	Superior to the Japanese Zero. Hellcats shot down over 5,000 Japanese aircraft in the Second World War. Over 12,000 were built.
F7F Tigercat	November 1943	Twin-engined fighter that missed combat in the Second World War but saw service as a ground attack aircraft and night fighter in the Korean War.
F8F Bearcat	August 1944	Grumman's last propeller fighter. Powerful and fast, it set a climb-to-altitude record to 10,000ft of 94 seconds that remained for ten years until being broken by a jet.
F9F Panther	November 1947	Grumman's first jet fighter. Saw much service in Korean War as a ground-attack aircraft.
F9F/F9 Cougar	September 1951	Swept-wing and more powerful version of Panther. Two-seat versions were used in Vietnam War.
XF10F-1 Jaguar	May 1952	Intended to give pilots lower landing and take-off speeds through its innovative wing-sweep mechanism, there were too many problems and it was abandoned.
F11F Tiger	July 1954	US Navy's first supersonic aircraft. Although in operational use for four years, was used by Blue Angels aerobatic team for eleven years.
F-14 Tomcat	December 1970	The Tomcat was a long-range fighter armed with the AIM-54 Phoenix missile, capable of firing at targets 100 miles away. Latterly used as the 'Bombcat'. Grumman's last Navy fighter retired in 2006.

GULF WAR AIRCRAFT

The first Gulf War in 1991 saw a large RAF presence. Many aircraft were decorated with names and nose art, some in the tradition of underdressed women, others with more of a modern theme, including characters from the adult humour comic *Viz*.

Buccaneer

Each aircraft had a nickname, a woman's name and a brand of Scotch whisky:

Guinness Girl/Pauline/The Macallan; Hello Sailor/Caroline/Famous Grouse; Jaws/Lynn/Glenfiddich; Laser Lips/Laura/Linkwood; Miss Jolly Roger/Fiona/Glenfarclas; Sea Witch/Debbie/Tamnavoulin; The Flying Mermaid/Kathryn/Glen Elgin.

Jaguar

Buster Gonad, Debbie, Diplomatic Service, Fat Slags, Johnny Fartpants, Katrina Jane, Mary Rose, Sadman, The Guardian Reader.

Tornado

Alarm Belle, Amanda-Jane, Anna Louise, Anola Kay, Armoured Charmer, Awesome Annie, Black Magic, Buddha, Check Six, Cherry Lips, Dhahran Annie, Fire Dancer, Flying High, Foxy Killer, Gulf Killer, Hello Kuwait G'bye Iraq, Luscious Lizzie, Maid Marian, Mig Eater, Miss Behavin, Snoopy Airways/Debbie, Snoopy Airways/Emma, Snoopy Airways/ Helen, Snoopy Airways/Nikki (Nora Batty), Triffid Airways, Where Do You Want It?

Nimrod

Battle Star 42, Guernsey's Girl.

Hercules

Betty Boob, Dennis the Menace: 'Let me at him!', Garfield: 'Where's the Beach?', Sid the Sexist: *The Silver Tounged [sic] Cavalier, The [Red] Baron.*

Tristar

The A Team, The Pink Panther.

VC10

The Empire Strikes Back.

Victor

Lucky Lou, Lusty Lindy, Maid Marian, Saucy Sal, Slinky Sue (Sweet Sue), Teasin' Tina.

H IS FOR...

HAPPY BOTTOM RIDING CLUB

The Happy Bottom Riding Club – also known as the Rancho Oro Verde Fly-Inn Dude Ranch – was a restaurant/bar/hotel set up close to the flight testing base situated in the Mojave Desert called Muroc Field, later named Edwards Air Force Base. The bar was owned and run by a remarkable woman: Florence 'Pancho' Barnes. Barnes' life reads like a Hollywood movie, which is entirely appropriate as for a time she was involved in organising stunt pilots for movies such as *The Flying Fool*. Barnes' interesting life included escaping her parents by marrying a church minister, having a son then leaving before ending up in South America on a Mexican gun-running boat. It was during this period she gained her nickname.

Barnes' interest in flying saw her taking part in air races and gaining speed records before the Great Depression wiped out most of her money. Fond of fun and hosting wild parties she then moved to the Mojave Desert where the club was established at her ranch. It was the only drinking establishment for hundreds of miles and test pilots like Chuck Yeager would socialise there. Pilots who broke the sound barrier for the first time were treated to a free steak dinner. In the 1950s the air force banned enlisted men from visiting the club on moral grounds and attempted to close down the ranch in order to clear ground for a proposed new runway (which was never built). A fire destroyed the ranch and despite being married four times, Barnes died alone in 1975.[22]

HEADLINES

Dayton Boys Solve Problem.
Wilbur and Orville Wright Successfully
Operate a Flying Machine in North Carolina.

Dayton Herald, 18 December 1903

Monument overlooking the location where Alcock and Brown landed, near Clifden. (Norman Ferguson)

The 'Dayton Boys' certainly had. The two brothers, Orville and Wilbur, who lived in Dayton, Ohio, had made four controlled flights from the beach at Kill Devil Hills, ushering in a new era in human transportation.[23]

> Bleriot Flies Across Channel,
> And Takes World by Surprise.
> Monoplane Attains Great Speed.
>
> *Evening Telegraph*, 26 July 1909

Bleriot's 36-minute-flight was the first to cross the English Channel in a powered flying machine. His Bleriot monoplane made a heavy landing but the Frenchman was unhurt.[24]

British Fliers Off on Big Hop Today.
Vickers-Vimy Plane All Ready For Start.
Captain Alcock And Lieutenant Brown Confident
They Will Succeed Where Hawker Failed.
Big Machine in Fine Shape.

The Boston Post, 13 June 1919

The British pair of John Alcock and Arthur Whitten Brown took off from Newfoundland on 14 June and 16 hours later landed in a bog near Clifden on the west coast of Ireland. They were the first to make a non-stop aerial crossing of the Atlantic and won the £10,000 prize offered by a newspaper for the first crossing within seventy-two hours. Their rival, Harry Hawker, with navigator Kenneth Mackenzie Grieve, had failed a month previously when the overheating engine of their Sopwith Atlantic forced them to ditch in the Atlantic Ocean. They were awarded £5,000 as a consolation prize.

Lindbergh Does It!
To Paris in 33½ hours;
Flies 1,000 Miles Through Snow and Sleet;
Cheering French Carry Him Off Field

The New York Times, 22 May 1927

Lindbergh's epic first solo aerial crossing of the Atlantic saw him receive global recognition. It was estimated that 100,000 welcomed him when he touched down in Paris; 500 had seen him take off a day and a half before.

Amelia Earhart Flies Atlantic,
First Woman To Do It;
Tells Her Own Story of Perilous 21-Hour Trip to Wales;
Radio Quit and They Flew Blind Over Invisible Ocean

The New York Times, 19 June 1928

Earhart became the first woman to fly across the Atlantic when she accompanied pilot Wilmer 'Bill' Stultz and mechanic Lou 'Slim' Gordon in the Fokker F.VII tri-motor seaplane, *Friendship*. They landed at Burry Port, Wales, after taking off from Newfoundland twenty hours and forty minutes before. Among the crowds who went to meet the intrepid flyers was a man who knew all about crossing the Atlantic in an aircraft: Sir Arthur Whitten Brown, and who lived in Wales. However, Brown was unsuccessful in finding them in the chaotic scenes that saw Earhart and companions take refuge in a zinc factory.[25]

RAF C-130 Hercules dropping paratroopers over Salisbury Plain in 2014. (MoD/ Crown copyright 2014)

A Great Achievement

The Scotsman, 26 May 1930

Amy Johnson was the first woman pilot to fly solo from the UK to Australia, a feat she accomplished in a de Havilland DH.60 Gipsy Moth called *Jason*. The flight took nineteen days.

First Flight of Jet Air-Liner.
Comet's Striking Performance.

The Times, 28 July 1949

The Comet was the world's first jet airliner and coming only four years after the end of the Second World War was a sign of Britain's determination to play an important role in commercial aviation.

HERCULES

The C-130 Hercules was designed by US manufacturer Lockheed as a medium-sized passenger and cargo transporter. It first flew in 1954. Over 2,500 have been built and manufacture continues, in the world's longest consecutive production run for a military aircraft.

It has been bought by almost seventy countries and its versatility, short take-off and landing performance (it remains the biggest aircraft to have flown off an aircraft carrier) has seen it used for the following roles:

- Airborne laser testing
- Air-to-air refuelling tanker
- Cargo transporter (civil and military)
- Command and control centre
- Electronic warfare
- Fire fighting
- Gunship
- Humanitarian relief
- Maritime patrol
- Medical evacuation
- Paratroop carrier
- Psychological warfare
- Reconnaissance
- Search and rescue
- Special forces carrier
- Weather observation[26]

HOLLYWOOD

Aviation provided an ideal subject matter for the early moviemakers. It was not difficult to find material for the big screen among the real-life human drama of the intrepid aviators. These films were some of those produced by Hollywood in the Golden Age of Aviation:

Title	Year Released	Leading Actors
Air Mail	1932	Ralph Bellamy, Pat O'Brien, Gloria Stuart
China Clipper	1936	Pat O'Brien, Humphrey Bogart
Ceiling Zero	1936	James Cagney, Pat O'Brien

Dirigible	1931	Jack Holt, Ralph Graves, Fay Wray
Hell's Angels	1930	Jean Harlow
Hell Divers	1931	Clark Gable, Wallace Beery
Men With Wings	1938	Fred MacMurray, Ray Milland, Louise Campbell
Only Angels Have Wings	1939	Cary Grant, Jean Arthur, Rita Hayworth
Tail Spin	1939	Alice Faye, Constance Bennett, Nancy Kelly
Test Pilot	1938	Clark Gable, Spencer Tracy, Myrna Loy
The Dawn Patrol	1930	Richard Barthelmess, Douglas Fairbanks Jnr
The Dawn Patrol	1938	David Niven, Errol Flynn, Basil Rathbone
The Eagles and the Hawk	1933	Fredric March, Cary Grant, Carole Lombard
The Flying Fleet	1929	Ramon Navarro, Ralph Graves, Anita Page
Wings	1927	Clara Bow, Charles 'Buddy' Rogers, Richard Arlen, Gary Cooper
Wings in the Dark	1935	Cary Grant, Myrna Loy
West Points of the Air	1935	Wallace Beery, Robert Young, Lewis Stone, Maureen O'Sullivan[27]

THE HOPPER

The nickname given to aviator and aircraft designer A.V. Roe by onlookers who gathered at Lea Marshes in Essex, to watch him attempt to take to the air. He eventually managed it and on 13 July 1909 became the first Briton to fly an all-British machine. His company Avro went on to build iconic aircraft such as the Lancaster and Vulcan bombers.

THE HUMAN FLY

Clay Lacy carried out many different types of flight in his long career as a business jet, airliner and jet fighter pilot but his most unusual was that performed at the request of The Human Fly, a character played by Canadian stuntman Rick Rojatt.

Rojatt asked Lacy if he could stand on top of a Learjet, but Lacy suggested using a Douglas DC-8 four-engined airliner. Rojatt agreed and several flights were made, with the costumed Rojatt standing on top of the fuselage, on the biggest wing-walking vehicle ever used. During a flight in Texas, he received injuries from heavy raindrops, which he described as being 'like bullets'. Rojatt later retired after a serious motorcycle accident.

I IS FOR...

I-SPY

I-SPY a delta wing with a projecting fuselage, and single sweptback fin. The four jet engines are completely enclosed in the wing and their tail-pipes are just visible at the trailing edge. Only two Vulcans are flying at present. There are a number of smaller delta aircraft in use for experimental flight testing and so you can make your I-SPY score for spotting any delta (other than the Javelin).

Entry for Avro Vulcan in 1950s book *I-SPY Aircraft*

Other aircraft illustrated in the book to be ticked off when seen by keen-eyed spotters:

Airspeed Ambassador
Auster
Avro Anson
Avro Shackleton
Avro Vulcan
Bristol Freighter
Bristol Type 173
de Havilland Dove and Heron
de Havilland Dragon Rapide
de Havilland Chipmunk
de Havilland Comet
de Havilland Tiger Moth
de Havilland Vampire and Venom
Douglas Dakota
English Electric Canberra
Fairey Gannet

Gloster Javelin
Gloster Meteor
Handley Page Hermes
Hawker Hunter
Hawker Sea Hawk
Lockheed Constellation
Lockheed Shooting Star
Miles Magister
North American Sabre
Percival Provost
Supermarine Attacker
Vickers Valiant
Vickers Viking
Vickers Viscount
Westland Wyvern

ICE PILOTS

From its beginnings in 1970 the Canadian operator Buffalo Airways has always flown several aircraft from a bygone era such as Douglas DC-3s, DC-4s and Curtiss C-46s. Featured in reality TV show *Ice Pilots NWT* these piston-engined machines carry freight and passengers and ones such as the DC-4 are equipped to drop retardant onto forest fires.

ICELAND DC-3s

When an Icelandic Airlines Douglas C-54 Skymaster force landed on Iceland's Vatnajökull glacier in September 1950, a US Air Force C-47 (the military version of the Douglas DC-3) flew out to rescue the crew.

This C-47 was equipped with skis in place of the normal wheeled undercarriage but it got stuck in the ice, and the crew were all evacuated. The C-47 was soon buried by snow and was abandoned by the air force.

The aircraft remained in the glacier until April 1951 when the owners of Icelandic Airlines bought it for $600 and set about digging the aircraft out. After it emerged from the snow it looked intact and was dragged 60 miles by tractor to flatter ground. Those involved in the salvage were pleasantly surprised to see both engines start up. The plane was flown out to Reykjavik and later sold to Spanish airline Iberia for $75,000.

The wrecks of two DC-3s remain on Iceland, one a US Navy R4D-8 version which force landed on the beach at Sólheimasandur in the south of the island in 1973. Its empty fuselage is now a favourite tourist destination. The other wreck came about when a R4D-6 was damaged during a take off at Thórshöfn in July 1969. It was abandoned on site.[28]

IMPERIAL AIRWAYS

In 1924 four British airlines (Handley Page Transport, Instone Air Line, Daimler Airway, British Marine Air Navigation Company) were merged into a new company: Imperial Airways. Aircraft used by Imperial Airways were often named, many reflecting the destinations of this empire-spanning airline. Imperial Airways became part of the British Overseas Airways Corporation in 1940.

Imperial Airways Named Aircraft:

Airco DH.4
City of York

Armstrong Whitworth Argosy
City of Glasgow
City of Birmingham
City of Wellington (later City of Arundel)
City of Edinburgh
City of Liverpool
City of Manchester
City of Coventry

Armstrong Whitworth AW.15 Atalanta
Atalanta (later Arethusa)
Amalthea
Atalanta
Andromeda
Artemis
Aurora
Astraea
Athena

Armstrong Whitworth Ensign
Ensign
Egeria
Elsinore
Euterpe
Explorer
Eddystone
Ettrick
Empyrean
Elysian
Euryalus
Echo
Endymion

Avro 10
Achilles
Apollo

Avro 652 (Anson)
Avalon
Avatar (later Ava)

Boulton Paul P.71A
Boadicea
Britomart

de Havilland DH.91 Albatross
Frobisher
Falcon
Fortuna
Fingal
Fiona

de Havilland DH.66 Hercules
City of Cairo
City of Delhi
City of Baghdad
City of Jerusalem
City of Teheran
City of Basra
City of Karachi
City of Jodhpur
City of Cape Town

de Havilland DH.86B
Delphinus
Delia
Daedalus
Draco
Dorado

Imperial Airways HP.42 *Hanno* refuelling at Semakh in Palestine. (Library of Congress, Prints & Photographs Division, LC-M3201-4239)

<u>Handley Page W.8b</u>
Princess Mary
Prince George
Prince Henry

<u>Handley Page Hamilton</u>
City of Washington

<u>Handley Page Hampstead</u>
City of New York

<u>Handley Page HP.42</u>
Hannibal
Horsa

Hanno
Hadrian
Heracles
Horatius
Hengist
Helena

<u>Handley Page W.10</u>
City of Melbourne
City of Pretoria
City of London
City of Ottawa

Short L.17 Scylla
Scylla
Syrinx

Short S.8 Calcutta
City of Alexandria
City of Athens (later *City of*
  Stonehaven)
City of Rome .
City of Khartoum
City of Salonika (later *Swanage)*

Short S.17 Kent
Scipio
Sylvanus
Satyrus

Short S.23 Empire flying boat
Canopus
Caledonia
Centaurus
Cavalier
Cambria
Castor
Cassiopeia
Capella
Cygnus
Capricornus
Corsair
Courtier
Challenger
Centurion
Coriolanus
Calpurnia
Ceres
Clio
Circe
Calypso
Camilla

Corinna
Cordelia
Cameronian
Corinthian
Coogee
Corio
Coorong
Carpentaria
Coolangatta
Cooee

Short S.26 G-Class flying boat
Golden Hind
Golden Fleece
Golden Horn[29]

Short S.30 Empire flying boat
Champion
Cabot
Caribou
Connemara
Clyde
Cathay
Captain Cook
Clare
Cumberland

Short S.33 Empire flying boat
Clifton
Cleopatra

Short-Mayo Composite (Short
S.20 seaplane and S.21 flying
boat)
Maia
Mercury

Vickers Vimy Commercial
City of London

INAPPROPRIATE NAMES

While some aircraft have been given names that sum up notions of aerial excellence and grace such as the Constellation, the Stratoliner, or others like the Spitfire or Thunderbolt conjure up warlike qualities, others might not strike the aviation-minded person as being particularly suited:

- Aeronca Chum
- Armstrong Whitworth Armadillo
- Armstrong Whitworth Ape
- Aviation Traders Accountant
- BAT Baboon
- BAT Bantam
- Blackburn Kangaroo
- de Havilland Dormouse
- Hawker Hedgehog
- Martinsyde Semi-quaver
- Parnall Elf
- Parnall Possum
- Pobjoy Pirate
- Saunders-Roe Skeeter
- Short Cockle
- Sopwith Gnu
- Sopwith Hippo
- Vickers Vildebeest
- Westland Witch
- Westland Wizard[30]

INCH

On 9 November 1962 test pilot Jack McKay had launched as normal from the B-52 carrier aircraft in a North American X-15 high-speed research aircraft. There was a problem with the rocket motor and so an emergency landing had to be made on the dry lakebed at Mud Lake, one of the areas specified for such events. McKay jettisoned as much fuel as he could but when the X-15 touched down it still had 1,000lb on board. The landing flaps had also failed and so the landing speed was higher than normal. The effect on touch down was to break one of the landing skids and when the wing hit the desert floor the X-15 turned over. McKay had jettisoned the cockpit canopy but this meant his head was exposed and it came into contact with the ground when the rocket plane stopped upside down. When the emergency vehicles got to the upturned aircraft they had to dig him out. He suffered crushed vertebrae and had lost one inch in height. McKay returned to flying the X-15 but the effects of his accident shortened his life and he died in 1975 aged 52.[31]

J IS FOR...

JACQUELINE COCHRAN

Cochran was the first woman to fly supersonically, which she did in 1953 flying a North American F-86 Sabre. Cochran had been a famous pilot in the 1930s, setting speed, distance and altitude records and winning events such as the Bendix Air Race in 1938.

During the Second World War Cochran lobbied to have women pilots play a role in the war effort and became director of the WASP (Women's Airforce Service Pilots) – the USA's equivalent of the United Kingdom's Air Transport Auxiliary. Cochran continued in aviation after the war and also took part in the Mercury 13 project to evaluate women's suitability for flying in space. She died in 1980.

JAMES BOND'S DESIGNER

The James Bond movies of the 1960s and 1970s are famous for their eye-catching set designs: the space port inside a volcano of *You Only Live Twice*, the interior of Fort Knox in *Goldfinger* and the inside of a super tanker holding nuclear submarines in *The Spy Who Loved Me*.

They were all the creations of production designer Ken Adam, born Klaus Hugo Adam in Germany in 1921, who was one of the few Germans to fly with the RAF during the Second World War. Adam flew with 609 Squadron flying the tank-busting Hawker Typhoon during the advance through Western Europe in the latter stages of the war. Born a Jew he would have been executed if shot down.

B-47 JATO-assisted take-off. (USAF)

JAMES McCUDDEN

James McCudden was one of the great pilots of the First World War. He began as a mechanic but found his true vocation in the air, where he shot down fifty-seven aircraft. McCudden recorded his experiences in a book written during the war called *Flying Fury: Five Years in the Royal Flying Corps*. One incident he recounted in February 1917 gives an indication of the type of event encountered in the air over the Western Front:

On the 16th I led my patrol out and flew down the trenches from Arras, as the clouds were only at 5,000ft, and Archie was too much respected in that sector for us to take liberties with him. By the time we had got down to Monchy (by the way, the Roland which I had shot down the day before still lay where it fell) I saw two Huns attacking a BE over Gommecourt. Whilst hastening to his assistance I saw one Hun go into a dive, then past the vertical on to his back, then into a vertical dive again, in which he stayed until he went through the roof of a house in Hebuterne with an awful whack and a lot of flying debris. The other Hun who was attacking the BE made off as fast as he possibly could, not wishing to share a similar fate. I thought at the time 'By Jove! That's the stuff to give the Hun'.

McCudden did not survive the war, being killed in a flying accident on 9 July 1918.

JASTAS AND JAGDGESCHWADEREN

In the First World War the aircraft provided to front-line units for military use quickly developed from the slow and lightly armed craft that saw service in 1914 to far more powerful machines specifically designed for warfare. As well as the aircraft, the organisations also saw changes. Squadrons at the beginning of the war contained a mix of types but this was done away with to have one squadron equipped with one type. Fighter squadrons were created with the aim of combating other aircraft in the skies. The German fighter units were called 'Jastas' – from Jagdstaffeln (hunting squadrons).

In June 1917 four Jastas were collected into a Jagdgeschwader (fighter wing) JG 1 – commanded by the Red Baron, Manfred von Richthofen, the war's leading ace. As JG 1 was moved around the Western Front to wherever it was required to combat Allied airpower it earned the name 'Richthofen's Traveling Circus' by the Royal Flying Corps.

While a squadron commander, von Richthofen had had his Albatros fighter painted bright red and he encouraged his squadron pilots to paint their machines in as colourful schemes as possible. It was useful for recognition while in the air and it also served as a way of proclaiming their presence in the aerial battlefield. The wing was credited with shooting down 644 Allied aircraft by the war's end.[32]

JATO

Jet Assisted Take-Off (also known as Rocket Assisted Take-Off) is where rockets attached to an aircraft's fuselage are used to shorten the take-off distance. Some of the aircraft to use JATO include:

Beech UC-45F Expeditor	2-engined propeller aircraft
Boeing 727	3-engined jet airliner
Boeing B-47 Stratojet	6-engined nuclear jet bomber

Dassault Mirage III	supersonic jet fighter
Dassault Mirage IV	supersonic nuclear jet bomber
Douglas B-66B Destroyer	2-engined jet bomber
Douglas D-558-II Skyrocket	jet and rocket-powered high-speed research aircraft
ERCO Ercoupe	single-engined light aircraft
Fairey Fulmar	single-engined propeller fighter
Hawker Hurricane	single-engined propeller fighter
Lockheed C-130 Hercules	4-engined propeller cargo transport
Lockheed F-104 Starfighter	single-engined supersonic fighter
Martin XB-51	prototype 3-engined jet bomber
Messerschmitt 323 Gigant	6-engined large propeller transporter

JOLLY GREEN GIANTS

Fighter pilots have no fear, Jolly Green Giants are always near.

Sign displayed at dispersal for 37th ARRS,
Da Nang, Vietnam

The 37th ARRS (Aerospace Rescue and Recovery Squadron) operated HH-3 nicknamed 'Jolly Green Giants' and HH-53 'Super Jolly Green Giants' in recovering downed airmen. Between 1962 and 1975 when all US involvement ceased, the US Air Force's rescue units had recovered 2,780 combat aircrew in South-East Asia.

K IS FOR...

KAL 007

On 31 August 1983 Korean Air Lines Flight 007 took off from New York's John F. Kennedy International Airport, destined for South Korea. The flight would route via Anchorage, Alaska.

After it left Anchorage and crossed the Bering Sea the Boeing 747 was detected by the Soviet Union's military defence radars as it approached – then encroached – into Soviet airspace, flying over the Kamchatka Peninsula. The airliner was hundreds of miles off its correct course. As it headed towards Sakhalin Island it was intercepted by a Sukhoi Su-15 fighter that fired two missiles, one of which hit. The jet did not break up but slowly descended until crashing into the sea. All 269 passengers and crew on board were killed. The incident caused international outcry but was not the only occurence of civilian jets being brought down by military action.

In April 1978 Soviet fighters had brought down another Korean Air Lines jet, a Boeing 707, near Murmansk when it too strayed into Soviet airspace. It had left Paris for Seoul but when nearing Greenland the crew made a huge navigational error in turning the aircraft south-eastwards towards the Soviet Union. A Sukhoi Su-15 fired missiles at the jet and forced it to land on a frozen lake near the Finnish border. Two passengers were killed.

Other civilian aircraft include the Iran Air Airbus A300 shot down by the US Navy's warship USS *Vincennes* over the Persian Gulf on 3 July 1988. The *Vincennes* fired two surface-to-air missiles at what its crew claimed was an Iranian F-14. An investigation showed the airliner had been transmitting its correct civilian identification codes at the time of missile launch. All 290 crew and passengers were killed.

More recently on 17 July 2014 a Malaysia Airlines Boeing 777 was flying over Ukraine when it was hit by a Russian-made surface-to-air missile. All 283 on board were killed.

KAMIKAZE

One of the grimmest aspects of aviation is the suicide attack. Seen to devastating effect in September 2001, this type of offensive action was first seen in the Second World War. The German aviator Hanna Reitsch had supported the use of a suicide squadron in the Luftwaffe using converted V-1 flying bombs and some German pilots flew suicide attacks against the Soviet Union forces late in the war. However, it was in the Pacific War where Japanese *Kamikaze* (Divine Wind) units were organised and used in far greater numbers. The first major attacks were in October 1944 during the Battle of Leyte Gulf, and a Zero fighter sank the American aircraft carrier *St Lo* on 25 October. Almost 4,000 Japanese pilots were lost and at times the Allies faced 300 attacks a day. The sheer scale of the resources available to the Allies eventually defeated the Kamikazes, as Japan ran out of men, and time.[33]

Hawker Sea Fury at Leuchars Air Show in 2013. (Norman Ferguson)

KIDDO

On 15 October 1910 the airship *America* left its shed in Atlantic City for an attempt on the first aerial transatlantic crossing. On board were six men, and one cat, brought on board by the airship's navigator. Once in the air Kiddo the cat did not relish the flight and started causing a disturbance. Fed-up engineer Melvin Vaniman made the first air-to-ground radio transmission when he broadcast to the ship towing *America* out to its launching position: 'Roy, come and get this goddamn cat!'

He tried to get rid of Kiddo by lowering him in a bag to the ship underneath but the seas were too rough and he was kept on board. Kiddo settled down and survived when the flight was abandoned after 72 hours, and the crew were picked up a passing ship. The *America* was still complete but was blown by the wind out of sight.

Kiddo was fêted on reaching New York and put on show in a department store window. Vaniman died on the *Akron* accident of 1912. Another transatlantic airship cat was *Whoopsie* who flew in the R34 in 1919 on its transatlantic flights.[34]

KNIGHTS OF THE AIR

Pilots in the First World War were a new element in warfare and, operating high above the battlefield engaged in one-to-one combat, they were seen as a noble embodiment of medieval chivalry, being called 'knights of the air'. Throughout the war there were occurrences when episodes showed a reflection of the code of behaviour from earlier times: at the start of the war, when aircraft were not always armed, airmen would salute each other when passing close by, or when a renowned ace would be killed, wreaths would be dropped by the other side as a mark of respect. But the First World War was not generally a place for high-minded chivalry and efficient killing tactics became the order of the day, especially for the high-scoring aces who mastered the lethal art of aerial combat, the main strand of which was to shoot without being seen and not to get entangled in a dangerous dogfight. French aviator Antoine de Saint-Exupery once wrote, 'Fighters don't kill, they murder.'

KOMET

The small, rocket-powered Messerschmitt Me163B Komet was well named – it climbed almost vertically, could reach speeds of around 620mph and altitudes of 40,000ft. The secret to its performance lay in two liquids: C-Stoff (Hydrazine hydrate, methanol and water) and T-Stoff (Hydrogen peroxide with hydro-carbon compounds). When combined they produced an explosive mixture – around four-fifths of Komets were lost due to explosions.

A pilot about to land had to ensure there was no fuel left in his tanks otherwise the impact could set off the remaining propellants. Another danger lay in the corrosive nature of the T-Stoff. One pilot who crashed but whose machine didn't explode was found dead inside his cockpit. He had been dissolved.

The Komet's size and speed made it difficult for Allied aircraft to shoot down but its effectiveness was reduced by its limited flight duration – 7 minutes' powered flight – and only nine Allied bombers are reported to have been shot down.[35]

KOREAN WAR

The Korean War was the first conflict to see jets heavily used. The Royal Australian Air Force operated Meteors, the US Air Force flew F-86

Sabres and F-80 Shooting Stars and the US Navy operated F9F Panthers. The North Koreans were equipped with Soviet-built MiG-15s.

Piston-engined aircraft were still in use however and one type, as flown by Lieutenant Peter 'Hoagy' Carmichael of the Royal Navy's Fleet Air Arm, made British aviation history on 9 August 1952.

Carmichael was flying a Hawker Sea Fury on a ground attack mission with three others from 802 Squadron when his formation were alerted to eight incoming MiG-15s. The Sea Furies turned to face their opponents and a dogfight ensued. Carmichael opened fire and was able to see his target being hit by his and other aircraft in his flight. It was seen to hit the ground. The remaining MiGs broke off their attack. This was the first occasion when a jet had been brought down by a British piston-engined aircraft.[36]

L IS FOR...

LAKE BENZIE

Lake Benzie, in Manitoba, Canada, is named in honour of a Canadian Battle of Britain pilot. Pilot Officer John Benzie was killed on 7 September 1940 when he was flying with 242 Squadron, at the time commanded by Douglas Bader.

LAST FLIGHTS

Concorde's Mach 2 speed, ability to fly at 60,000ft and delta-winged streamlined shape made it one of civil aviation's great aircraft. Following its first fatal crash in France in 2000, the decision was made to retire it. Air France retired theirs in May 2003 and British Airways announced that its machines would be taken out of service in October the same year. A series of flights to mark the occasion were made, in the USA and around the UK and on the last day of Concorde operations – 24 October 2003 – three Concordes made flights, which were scheduled to arrive back at their London Heathrow base at the same time. The unique sight of three Concordes lining up on approach at the same time was memorable to all who witnessed it.

Arrival Time	Aircraft	Pilot	Departure Airport
4.01 p.m.	G-BOAE	Les Brodie	Edinburgh
4.03 p.m.	G-BOAF	Paul Douglas	Heathrow (trip via Bay of Biscay)
4.05 p.m.	G-BOAG	Mike Bannister	John F. Kennedy, New York

LE MANS

On 8 August 1908 Wilbur Wright demonstrated at Hunaudières racetrack outside Le Mans in France, as part of a European visit to show off the flying machine made by him and his brother Orville. There had been doubts from European sceptics about the aerial effectiveness of the Americans' craft since their first flight in 1903 was made public. Some called them 'bluffers'. After the flight, *The Times* newspaper's Special Correspondent telegrammed a brief report, which was printed on 10 August 1908:

> Mr Wilbur Wright has made a remarkable flight this evening, lasting 1 minute 45 seconds, over a course of about 2,500ft. He will resume his experiments on Monday. The average height maintained during today's flight was 30 feet.

Wright's demonstration in the Wright Flyer silenced the doubters immediately and he received an enthusiastic response from those watching, which included French aviation pioneer Louis Bleriot who said, 'I consider that, for us in France and everywhere, a new era in mechanical flight has begun. I am not sufficiently calm after the event thoroughly to express my opinion. My view can best be conveyed in the words – it is marvellous.'

The Wrights' success stemmed from years of work put in to develop their own skills and adapt any lessons learnt to new aircraft. This took them ahead of their rivals, whose aircraft were only capable of straight-ahead flight; the Wright brothers' craft could turn.[37]

LEXINGTON

On 2 October 1957 Londoners watched as the word 'Lexington', a human face and a telephone number appeared in the sky. They were the work of two Harvards, operated by the Overseas Aviation, a company who specialised in skywriting. The skywriting was done around 13,000ft and at speeds just over 100mph. Lexington was a brand of cigarettes and the phone number was that of the sky writing company.[38]

LINDBERGH

How clearly I remember it. A silver gleam suddenly appeared out of the darkness of the night, passed over the field like a comet and then returned, gently gliding to the ground. There was a moment of calm and suspense until the vast crowd realized just what had happened. Then a roar like the breaking of a great dam and the flood swept everything before it. Iron fences, soldiers, police and everything else went down as the crowd poured over the field and swirled about the *Spirit of St Louis* like a whirlpool.

This was Myron T. Herrick, US Ambassador to France, writing about the arrival of Charles Lindbergh at Le Bourget airfield on 21 May 1927. Lindbergh's night-time arrival (he touched down at 10.24 p.m.) was greeted with huge and ecstatic crowds, who had been following his progress during the day.

Lindbergh's dramatic arrival was the climax to an epic flight. He had flown 3,614 miles non-stop from New York, battling tiredness the whole time. His flight of 33 hours, 30 minutes was the first transatlantic crossing completed by a solo flier and it pushed Lindbergh up into the heady heights of fame.

LOCOMOTIVES

After the war Southern Railway began naming forty-four of its locomotives in honour of the Battle of Britain. They were named after people, airfields, squadrons and organisations who took part:

17 Squadron	*229 Squadron*
25 Squadron	*249 Squadron*
41 Squadron	*253 Squadron*
46 Squadron	*257 Squadron*
66 Squadron	*264 Squadron*
73 Squadron	*501 Squadron*
74 Squadron	*601 Squadron*
92 Squadron	*602 Squadron*
141 Squadron	*603 Squadron*
145 Squadron	*605 Squadron*
213 Squadron	*615 Squadron*
219 Squadron	*Anti-Aircraft Command*
222 Squadron	*Biggin Hill*

Croydon
Fighter Command
Fighter Pilot
Hawkinge
Hurricane
Kenley
Lord Beaverbrook
Lord Dowding
Manston

Royal Observer Corps
Sir Archibald Sinclair
Sir Frederick Pile
Sir Keith Park
Sir Trafford Leigh-Mallory
Spitfire
Tangmere
Winston Churchill

LOST

During what is regarded as a golden period for British aviation in the early to mid-1950s, aircraft manufacturers came up with many different designs. Some were experimental while others were aimed at production. Some from this period such as the Victor, Vulcan and Lightning made it into long-term RAF service but others did not. Aircraft with great potential that were cancelled included:

Armstrong Whitworth AW.681

In the early 1960s there was a need to replace the RAF Support Command's Beverley and Hastings large transport aircraft. The proposed new aircraft was radically different from these four-engined propeller aeroplanes. The AW.681 was to have four jet engines and be capable of short take-off and landing with a load of 20 tons. With lift-jets added in pods to the wings vertical take-offs and landing were proposed. As with the TSR-2, the AW.681 was cancelled by the Labour government in 1965 and the RAF received American C-130 Hercules transport aircraft instead.[39]

BAC TSR-2

Perhaps the most often cited 'lost' aircraft. Designed to be a long-range, low-level supersonic bomber and reconnaissance aircraft the TSR-2 faced opposition due to technical failures and its high cost. It also suffered from in-service rivalry from ex-Royal Navy officer Lord Mountbatten, Britain's Chief of Defence Staff. It was scrapped in 1966 by the incoming Labour government and was to be replaced by the American F-111 but this fell through and the RAF were given Blackburn Buccaneers, which had been designed as low-level bombers for the Royal Navy.

Hawker Siddeley P.1121

The P.1121 was designed as a single-engined Mach 2.5 air superiority fighter with attack capability. Depending on the role it could be armed with air-to-air missiles, 30mm cannons, free-fall conventional and also nuclear weapons. The designers had evaluated that if upgraded it could fly at Mach 3. However, the Conservative government of 1957 implemented a policy change that envisaged a huge reduction in the requirement for manned fighter aircraft and the project never left the ground. A two-seat version the P.1129 was proposed for the operational requirement that saw the TSR.2 project.

Hawker Siddeley P.1154

The innovation produced by British aircraft manufacturers had been demonstrated in 1960 with the first flight of the Hawker Siddeley P.1127, a small single-engined jet aircraft (subsequently developed into the Kestrel) that was able to land and take off vertically, through the clever use of swivelling its engine's four nozzles. However, because it depended on having a high thrust-to-weight ratio in order to get into the sky, its fuel and weapon load was severely limited.

A development was planned, called the P.1154, which aimed to be supersonic, while also retaining vertical landing and take-off capability. It would equip both RAF and the Royal Navy squadrons with the RAF version being a strike aircraft while the navy's focused on interception. There were problems in trying to marry the two forces' aims in one aircraft but this was all cast aside when in 1965 the Labour government cancelled the project. The RAF went on to be equipped with the subsonic development of the P.1127 – the Harrier – and received the Royal Navy's choice of the F-4 Phantom.

Miles M-52

The Miles M.52 was designed to reach 1,000mph at altitudes above 30,000ft. It was conceived during the Second World War as a research aircraft to test high-speed flight but the project was mysteriously cancelled in 1946 before a full-scale prototype could be flown. Miles' machine featured an all-moving tail plane, which was adopted by the USA (in a one-way technology transfer) in its Bell X-1 experimental aircraft, which was first to break the sound barrier in 1947.

LUCKY ESCAPES

Luck has its place in aviation as with any other endeavour and as a result some pilots are superstitious – for example Second World War Hawker Typhoon pilot Desmond Scott carried a small pink glass elephant. He suffered extreme anxiety when he flew without his lucky charm. Scott survived the war.

Avro Anson

Mid-air collisions are terrifying events and normally result in the damage or destruction of the aircraft involved. It is highly unusual for both aircraft to be brought back to earth while conjoined as a result of their enforced aerial mating but incredibly this happened several times during the Second World War. One of these took place in 1940 in Australia when the Avro Anson twin-engined training aircraft flown by LAC Leonard Fuller impacted another Anson and became the upper part of a newly formed twin aircraft. The two occupants of the lower machine bailed out, as did his observer, but Fuller found he was able to control the two aircraft and carried out a successful landing. He was later killed in a road accident in 1944.[40]

BA Flight 38

On 17 January 2008, as British Airways Boeing 777 G-YMMM made its final approach to London's Heathrow airport there were no indications that anything untoward was about to happen. It had been in the air for 10½ hours since taking off from Beijing. As the airliner descended below 800ft the co-pilot John Coward took control. As the aircraft continued to descend, power to the engines started to reduce, and despite manual intervention by pushing the throttles forward, the aircraft started to slow down. The large wide-body airliner was now virtually gliding. The 180-ton machine just managed to cross the perimeter fence before landing heavily on the grass, 330 metres before the start of the runway. All of the aircraft's undercarriage legs gave way under the impact. All on board were able to evacuate safely; luckily there was no resulting fire.

Kvochur at Paris

At the 1989 Paris Airshow the Soviet Union had surprised the world with its MiG-29 fighter. It was highly manoeuvrable and on a par if not above Western fighter aircraft. During a display flown by test pilot Anatoly Kvochur, the MiG performed a slow-speed, high angle of attack pass, that is, with the nose pointing up at a sharp angle above the direction of flight. During this part of the display, the right engine suffered a bird strike, and immediately lost power. The aircraft yawed to the right and lost height rapidly. Kvochur ejected outside the safety parameters of his ejector seat at only 300ft above the ground. He landed safely, unharmed save for a few bruises and cuts. So close was he to his doomed jet, his parachute was inflated by the blast of the explosion as the plane hit the ground.

Miracle on the Hudson

On 15 January 2009, US Airways Flight 1549 took off from New York's LaGuardia Airport. Routine was quickly forgotten as only two minutes into the flight the Airbus A320 flew into a flock of Canada Geese causing a double engine flameout. At 3,000ft, with no engine power, the airliner began to descend over the built-up area of New York. Captain Chesley 'Sully' Sullenberger, an experienced pilot with over 19,000 flying hours, took control of the plane from co-pilot Jeffrey Skiles with the words 'My aircraft'.

The two possible airfields to land at – LaGuardia or Teterboro in New Jersey – were quickly evaluated as being too far away. Sullenberger announced their destination: 'We're gonna be in the Hudson' and 208 seconds after the bird strike, that's where the airliner ditched. With strong currents taking the slowly sinking airliner down river, a successful evacuation saw all 150 passengers and five crew escape, to stand on the wings or get into the inflatable evacuation slides that doubled as life rafts. Luckily this Airbus, N106US, was one of the US Airways fleet that was equipped with survival equipment for ditching. Help soon arrived with ferry boats being first on the scene and all passengers were rescued safely; five had serious injuries.[41]

Neil Armstrong

The future moonwalker began his professional flying career with the US Navy, flying F9F Panthers off the aircraft carrier USS *Essex* during the Korean War. During one low-level attack mission, his jet flew into a cable barrier. Armstrong was able to control his jet, which was now missing a 6ft-long section of one of his wings, and flew it back so that he could eject over friendly territory.[42]

Partial Ejection

In 1991, a Grumman KA-6D Intruder tanker took off from the American aircraft carrier USS *Abraham Lincoln*. Not long into the flight, and while carrying out some porpoise manoeuvres to clear a problem with a fuel tank, the pilot, Lieutenant Mark Baden heard a loud bang and felt the cockpit depressurise. He looked to his right and saw that his navigator, Lieutenant Keith Gallagher, was halfway outside the aircraft – only Gallagher's legs remained inside the cockpit. The pilot took immediate action to slow the aircraft down and headed for the carrier. He landed on deck and was relieved to hear his colleague ask if they were on the flight deck. Gallagher's ejector seat had come loose and slid up the rails. In doing so it had released Gallagher's straps from the seat so during his ordeal, he wasn't secured to either the seat or the aircraft. As his arms had been flung back by the force of the slipstream it took months of recuperation until he was fit to fly again. His pilot was awarded the US Navy Air Medal.

Sukhoi at Paris

Ten years after the MiG-29 incident, another Russian state-of-the-art fighter jet ran into difficulties or more accurately, the ground. While

Captain Stricklin ejecting from his F-16. (USAF/ Staff Sgt Bennie J. Davis III)

performing its routine at the Paris Airshow, the Sukhoi Su-30MK was halfway through its display when it came too low after some descending spirals. The aircraft slowly floated towards the ground, and its tail scraped along the grass, breaking one of the jet pipes in the process. The Sukhoi didn't crash immediately but rose into the sky, clawing for height. Its renewed flight couldn't last long and the blue and white jet soon fell earthwards. The two crew members on board ejected safely.

Thunderbirds are Gone

The Thunderbirds are the United States Air Force demonstration team, renowned for precise formation flying. The team fly F-16 fighter jets and in September 2003, Captain Chris Stricklin took off in the team's No. 6 aircraft for a display at Mountain Home Air Force Base. From take off he pulled straight into a Split-S manoeuvre. This involved a steep climb, half roll, then half a loop before pulling up to continue in level flight. However, Stricklin did not leave enough room for the manoeuvre. Realising the aircraft was going to crash, he ejected, only 140ft above the ground – 0.8 seconds before impact. He survived uninjured, although the plane was destroyed. Stricklin was blamed for the accident and left the team.
Forty-seven of those on board suffered injuries, one a broken leg. The enquiry found that ice had formed in the fuel – the 777 had flown at high altitude while crossing Russia and Sweden – and it had restricted fuel flow to the engines.[43]

LUFTWAFFE UNITS

Hitler's air force had been a key part of the Blitzkreig tactics that had ensured victory in Poland in 1939 and then Western Europe in 1940. With France secured, the Luftwaffe's bombers prepared to attack Britain across the English Channel in the summer of 1940. Among the Heinkel, Junkers and Dornier-equipped units some had been given names alongside their unit numbers:

KG 1	'Hindenburg'	KG 30	'Adler' (Eagle)
KG 2	'Holzhammer'	KG 51	'Edelweiss'
KG 3	'Blitz' (Lightning)	KG 53	'Legion Condor'
KG 4	'General Wever'	KG 54	'Totenkopf'
KG 26	'Löwen' (Lion)		(Death's Head)
KG 27	'Boelcke'	KG 55	'Greif' (Griffin)

M IS FOR...

MANFRED VON RICHTHOFEN

Manfred von Richthofen was the First World War's highest-scoring ace, with eighty victories. In 1917 he wrote a book of his war experiences and included an account of an extended dogfight with British ace Major Lanoe Hawker that took place on 23 November 1916. Von Richthofen was flying a Fokker D.II and Hawker an Airco DH.2:

> The circles which we made around one another were so narrow that their diameter was probably no more than 250 or 300 feet. I had time to take a good look at my opponent. I looked down into his carriage and could see every movement of his head. If he had not had his cap on I would have noticed what kind of a face he was making.
>
> My Englishman was a good sportsman, but by and by the thing became a little too hot for him. He had to decide whether he would land on German ground or whether he would fly back to the British lines. Of course he tried the latter, after having endeavoured in vain to escape me by looping and such like tricks. At that time his first bullets were flying around me, for hitherto neither of us had been able to do any shooting.
>
> When he had come down to about three hundred feet he tried to escape by flying in a zig-zag course during which, as is well known, it is difficult for an observer to shoot. That was my most favourable moment. I followed him at an altitude of from two hundred and fifty feet to one hundred and fifty feet, firing all the time. The Englishman could not help falling. But the jamming of my gun nearly robbed me of my success.
>
> My opponent fell, shot through the head, one hundred and fifty feet behind our line. His machine-gun was dug out of the ground and it ornaments the entrance of my dwelling.
>
> *The Red Battle Flyer* by Manfred von Richthofen

Like many of the other aces, von Richthofen did not survive the war having been killed in April 1918.

MARGARET HORTON

It was common practice when Spitfires were taxiing out in high winds, for a member of the ground crew to sit on one of the tail planes, to counter the Spitfire's tendency to tip onto its nose.

On 14 February 1945 at RAF Hibaldstow, Spitfire AB910 was taxying out with Margaret Horton, a Women's Auxiliary Air Force fitter, sitting on the tail. This standard procedure was quickly rendered non-standard when pilot Neil Cox accelerated down the runway and took off, with his rear passenger still on the machine.

Through the sluggish nature of the controls – Horton was holding onto the elevator for grim life – Cox realised there was a problem and quickly returned and landed. During her short flight, Horton was certain she would not survive, and wondered who would get her rations. AB910 remains in flying condition with the RAF's Battle of Britain Memorial Flight.[44]

MASCOTS

Flying and superstitions have always gone together and aviators used a variety of ways of warding off bad luck: some pilots thought it unlucky to have their photograph taken before taking off and others trusted their continuing fortunes to physical items, such as mascots carried into the air with them:

Name/Item	Description	Period
'Adolphus'	Knitted toy dog flown by Major Maurice Leblanc-Smith, RFC.	WW1
'Bea'	Teddy bear, flown by Flight Lieutenant Stephen Beaumont of 609 Squadron in Battle of Britain.	WW2
'Eeyore'	Small soft toy character from *Winnie the Pooh*, carried in his Spitfire's cockpit by pilot Geoffrey Wellum in Battle of Britain.	WW2
Gremlins	Cloth figures, carried by RAF bomber crews to combat the evil 'Gremlins' that were believed to cause damage to aircraft.	WW2
Kangaroo	Made out of pipe cleaners and flown in RAF Lancaster R5868 'S' for Sugar. It certainly was lucky as no crew member was killed in any of the 137 missions this aircraft flew.	WW2
'Lucky Jim' and 'Twinkletoes'	Two toy cats carried on Alcock and Brown's transatlantic flight in 1919. They were given as charms by Brown's fiancée.	Inter-war
'Percy'	Penguin soft toy carried by Flight Lieutenant Stan Chapman of 158 Squadron. Chapman (and his penguin) were shot down and captured in 1944.[45]	WW2

| 'Teddy Cooper' | Carried on operations by flight engineer Frederick Cooper who survived the war. | WW2 |
| 'Tem' | Woollen doll flown on special operations over occupied France. | WW2 |

MAYFLIES

Two early flying craft were given the name *Mayfly*.

MAYFLY	Name	MAYFLY
Biplane	Type	Naval airship
Lilian Bland	Owner	Royal Navy
1910	Date made	1911
Near Belfast, Northern Ireland	Location	Cavendish Dock, Barrow-in-Furness, England
The first aircraft to be built and flown by a woman. There was no fuel tank ready for the first engine runs so a whisky bottle was used, connected by Bland's deaf aunt's ear trumpet. The *Mayfly* wasn't a huge success (it was underpowered and could only reach a height of 30ft). Bland's disapproving father offered to buy her a car if she'd give up flying and she emigrated to Canada in 1912 and played no further part in aviation. The aircraft was used as a glider by Dublin Flying Club.	Notes	His Majesty's Airship No. 1 was intended to be the United Kingdom's rival to the German Zeppelins. However, on 24 September 1911, the 512ft-long airship was damaged beyond repair when it broke in two while being manoeuvred outside its shed. First Lord of the Admiralty Winston Churchill called it the 'Won't Fly' and Admiral Sturdee, who was in charge of the accident's enquiry, said, on seeing the wreckage, it was 'the work of a lunatic'.[46]

MEMO

The War Office had decided to cease making any experiments with aeroplanes as the cost has proved too great … Aircraft are useless for army purposes as it was impossible for anybody moving at more than forty miles an hour to see anything at all.

War Office memo to Lieutenant J.W. Dunne and Colonel S.F. Cody in 1909. Cody had made the first powered aircraft flight in the United Kingdom and could see the advantages of heavier-than-air aircraft for military use. It would not be too long until all military commanders could also see the benefits.

USAF C-5 Galaxy. (Michael Pereckas/Flickr CC 2.0)

MESSAGE IN A BOTTLE

Nungesser-Coli, au secours.

This distress message (translated as 'Nungesser-Coli, help') was written on a small piece of paper found inside a glass bottle on 18 July 1927. A 14-year-old boy found it on the shore at Mike's Cove, Point May, Newfoundland. Nungesser and Coli were two French airmen who had taken off from Paris on 8 May 1927 to attempt to become the first to cross the Atlantic. After they launched they were never seen again.[47]

MIGHTY MACHINES

Antonov An-225 Mriya

Engines:	6 x ZMKB Progress Lotarev D-18T turbofans
Weight:	1,411,000lb (maximum take off weight)
Wingspan:	290ft
Length:	275ft
First flight:	21 December 1988

The Antonov An-225 is the world's biggest aircraft of which only one example was built. It was designed to carry the Soviet Union's space shuttle Buran but after that project was cancelled it is used for transporting very large cargo items.

Bristol Brabazon

Engines:	8 x Bristol Centaurus radial engines
Weight:	290,000lb (maximum take off weight)
Wingspan:	230ft
Length:	177ft
First flight:	4 September 1949

At the time this was the world's largest land-based aircraft. Orders weren't forthcoming and the project was cancelled in 1952.

Convair B-36 Peacemaker

Engines:	6 x R-4360 pistons, 4 x J-47-GE19 jets
Weight:	410,000lb (maximum take off weight)
Wingspan:	230ft
Length:	162ft
First flight:	8 August 1946

The giant B-36 was an American long-range intercontinental bomber able to drop nuclear weapons deep behind the Iron Curtain. It had a range of 7,500 miles when carrying 10,000lb of bombs. This monster of the skies was superseded by the B-47.

Lockheed C-5 Galaxy

Engines:	4 x General Electric TF39 turbofans
Weight:	840,000lb (maximum take off weight)*
Wingspan:	222ft*
Length:	247ft*
First flight:	30 June 1968

The Galaxy is the US military's largest aircraft, able to transport a 74-ton mobile bridge inside its cargo compartment. With a load of 120,000lb it can fly almost 5,000 miles. (*C-5B version)[48]

RAF Chinook
in Afghanistan.
(MoD/Crown
Copyright
2008, POA
(Photo:
Sean Clee)

Myasischev M-50 'Bounder'

Engines:	4 x Dobrynin VD-7 turbojets
Weight:	440,925lb (maximum take off weight)
Wingspan:	115ft
Length:	188ft
First flight:	27 October 1959

The USSR's Bounder (its NATO code name) was a supersonic intercontinental nuclear bomber which first flew in 1959. Looking like something a schoolboy would draw, it had a long thin fuselage with delta wings, and had an engine suspended below each wing and one on each wingtip.

MOTTOS OF THE RAF SQUADRON

One of the famous RAF squadron mottos is *Aprés moi, le déluge* ('After me, the flood') appropriately that of the Dambusters squadron, 617. Twenty others are:[49]

No.	Motto (Latin)	English translation
1(F)	*In omnibus princeps*	First in all things
II (AC)	-	Hereward (Guardian of the army)
3	*Tertius primus erit*	The third shall be the first
IV (R)	*In futurum videre*	To see into the future
5 (AC)	*Frangas non flectas*	Thou mayst break but shall not bend me
6	*Oculi exercitus*	The eyes of the army
7	*Per diem, per noctem*	By day and by night
8	*Uspiam et passim*	Everywhere unbounded
9	*Per noctum volamus*	Throughout the night we fly
10	*Rem acu tangere*	To hit the mark
11	*Ociores acrierosquaquilis*	Swifter and keener than eagles
12	-	Leads the Field
13	*Adjuvamus tuendo*	We assist by watching
14	-	I spread my wings and keep my promise
XV	-	Aim sure
16	*Operta aperta*	Hidden things are revealed
17	*Excellere contende*	Strive to excel

18	*Animo et fide*	With courage and faith
19	*Possunt quia posse videntur*	They can because they think they can
20	*Facta non verba*	Deeds not words

N IS FOR...

NATIVE AMERICAN NAMES

Helicopters used by the US Army and Air Force are named after Native American tribes or people:

- UH-1 Iroquois
- H-19 Chickasaw
- CH-37 Mojave
- H-34 Choctaw
- CH-54 Tarhe
- CH-47 Chinook
- H-21 Shawnee
- OH-58 Kiowa
- H-13 Sioux

- OH-6 Cayuse
- TH-55 Osage
- UH-60 Black Hawk
- AH-56 Cheyenne
- RAH-66 Comanche
- AH-64 Apache
- ARH-70 Arapaho
- UH-72 Lakota

NICKNAMES

Aircraft have been given nicknames since the early days of aviation, some affectionate and complimentary, others less so.

Airco DH.6[50]

This First World War two-seater trainer was an effective and safe aircraft. It had a minimum speed of 30mph and was difficult to stall, ideal for inexperienced pilots. Despite this it acquired several nicknames:

The Clockwork Mouse
The Clumsy Hearse
The Clutching Hand[51]

The Crab
The Dung Hunter
The Flying Coffin
The Sky Hook

Bognor Bloater

The White & Thompson biplane of 1915 acquired this uncomplimentary name due to where it had been built (Bognor Regis) and to the fish scales-like effect of the copper-coloured stitching on the fuselage.[52]

Bull's Eye

The AV Roe I triplane was called the Bull's Eye after a successful product made by designer AV Roe's brother's company – the Bullseye Braces – which helped finance his aeronautical ventures.[53]

Elephant

The Martinsyde G.100 First World War biplane bomber was called the Elephant because of its size and lack of manoeuvrability.

Flying Cathedral

Pioneer Samuel F. Cody's 43ft-wingspan biplane of 1911 was given this nickname due to its size, although it wasn't the largest aircraft of the time.[54]

Goldfish

The Royal Aircraft Factory BE.3 gained this name due to the shape of its tail plane.[55]

Spinning Incinerator

The First World War Airco DH.2 fighter was given this nickname because of its high accident rate when it was introduced.[56]

Yellow Peril

The Handley Page Type D monoplane gained this moniker from its colourful yellow and blue paint scheme. It was also called 'Antiseptic' due to the smell from the chemical treatment applied to the metalwork to prevent rusting.

9/11

The attacks of 11 September 2001 saw commercial airliners used as weapons in a devastating manner. Their destructive power stemmed from a combination of size, being heavily laden with fuel and being flown at high speed when they impacted:[57]

Speed at Impact	Flight Number	Aircraft Type	Target Site
465mph	American Airlines Flight 11	Boeing 767	World Trade Center North Tower, New York
530mph	American Airlines Flight 77	Boeing 757	Pentagon, Washington, DC
563mph	United Airlines Flight 93	Boeing 757	Shanksville, Pennsylvania
586mph	United Airlines Flight 175	Boeing 767	World Trade Center South Tower, New York

NOISE ABATEMENT PROCEDURE

In the 1970s there were protests in America by those concerned about an increase in aircraft noise pollution with the introduction of Concorde to transatlantic routes. To counter the effects of its four afterburning Olympus engines, a noise abatement procedure was added to Concorde's flight path when it took off from runway 31L at New York, JFK Airport:

- Take off (198 knots). Rotate to 13° climb angle (within 5 seconds).
- With rate of climb established at 500ft per minute, begin left turn, with 25° of bank (beginning around 50ft of altitude).
- At pre-determined point (approximately after 1 minute's flight-time) cancel reheat and pull back throttles to attain speed of 240–250 knots.
- Once passed 235° Magnetic, select full thrust (without reheat), reduce bank angle to 7.5°, at 250 knots.
- At 2,500ft, pull back throttles to present quadrant angle, keeping 250 knots.
- Once over the ocean full power to be applied.[58]

NORTH POLE

The man who first led a team to the South Pole on foot was also the first to fly over the North Pole. In 1926 Norwegian explorer Roald Amundsen and fifteen others took off from Ny-Alesund in Spitsbergen, off the north coast of Norway, in the airship *Norge* captained by Italian Umberto Nobile. Seventy-two hours later, despite encountering storm-force winds, they landed safely at Teller, Alaska.

Aerial Arctic exploration was no safer than land-based endeavours. A previous attempt by Amundsen using two Dornier flying boats turned into a story of survival when one of the aircraft was unable to continue and all his men had to dig a runway out of the snow and cram into the servieable machine, before flying back to Svalbard. Then in 1928 when Nobile and his crew went missing on another airship expedition, Amundsen set off on a rescue attempt but was never seen again.[59]

NOVELS

Although not a subject widely covered by novelists there have been some classic books written with aviation as the subject.

Night Flight (1931) by Antoine de Saint-Exupéry

This short novel combines an account of an aircraft carrying mail from Patagonia to Buenos Aires as its pilot and navigator encounter a storm, with that of the company's ground-based staff awaiting news of the aircraft's progress. The story, based on Saint-Exupery's own experiences, gives a sense of the pressures these early flyers and their employers experienced as they took on new roles in the skies.

No Highway (1948) by Nevil Shute

Shute had been a co-founder of the Airspeed aircraft manufacturing company and this novel centres on attempts by the Royal Aircraft Establishment at Farnborough to prove whether a new transatlantic airliner, the Rutland Reindeer, is safe to fly, or whether it has issues with metal fatigue that may have caused a fatal crash in Canada.

The High and the Mighty (1953) by Ernest K. Gann

Gann was another writer who was also a pilot, and he used his experiences flying airliners in his writing. This novel follows the sixteen passengers and five crew on an unnamed airliner on a journey across the Pacific from Hawaii to San Francisco. The routine flight is interrupted when an engine failure means they may have to ditch.

The Hunters (1956) by James Salter

This novel about American F-86 Sabre fighter pilots in the Korean War was written by a veteran of that war, whose experiences are mirrored in that of the main character: Cleve Connell. The desire for pilots to prove themselves by shooting down MiGs is a main theme. Connell attempts to carve his own reputation, competing against the enemy pilots and his own fellow squadron members.

Catch-22 (1961) by Joseph Heller

Joseph Heller served as a bomb aimer during the Second World War with the US Army Air Force. Heller's experience clearly influenced his writing, as the novel's main character is Yossarian, a B-25 bomb aimer whose squadron is taking part in the Italian campaign. Yossarian sees the insanity of war and attempts to escape, however his awareness of the madness shows he can't be insane and thus can't be classed as insane on medical grounds – a situation known as Catch-22. This deeply dark comic novel remains a constant in lists of all-time great novels.

O IS FOR...

OBJECTS CONFISCATED AT AIRPORTS

4ft-long squash (Birmingham, 2014)[60]
200 tarantulas (Schiphol, 2012)[61]
Ceramic cats full of opium (John F. Kennedy Airport, New York, 2011)[62]
Chameleon, worn as a hat (Manchester, 2002)[63]
Dried caterpillars (Gatwick, 2013)[64]
Human eyeballs (Stansted, 2007)[65]
Human skeleton (Munich, 2008)[66]
Pigeons, in padded envelopes on smuggler's calves (Melbourne, 2009)[67]
Songbirds strapped to smuggler's legs (Los Angeles, 2009)[68]
Tiger cub (alive in suitcase) (Bangkok, 2010)[69]

OCEANS AND SEA CROSSINGS

Louis Bleriot's crossing of the English Channel in 1909 was an epoch-making event, showing that the old geographical boundaries could no longer be viewed as before. Some were concerned that they were not vulnerable to a new type of threat. It also showed the opportunities that crossing of major areas of water presented. They served as crucial challenges to be met.

SEA/OCEAN	ROUTE	DATE	PILOT/CREW	AIRCRAFT	DURATION	NOTES
Irish Sea	Goodwick, near Fishguard, Pembrokeshire to Crane, County Wexford, Ireland	22 April 1912	Denys Corbett Wilson (solo)	Bleriot XI	1 hour 40 minutes	Corbett Wilson was killed in 1915 when his aircraft was hit by an artillery shell.
Mediterranean Sea	Fréjus, St Raphael, France to Bizerta, Tunisia	23 September 1913	Roland Garros (solo)	Morane-Saulnier monoplane	7 hours 53 minutes	Garros landed with just one gallon of fuel remaining from the 55 he took off with. He was later killed in the First World War. A keen tennis player, the national stadium in Paris was named in his honour.
North Sea	Cruden Bay, Aberdeenshire to Jaeren, near Stavanger, Norway	30 July 1914	Tryggve Gran (solo)	Bleriot XI-3 monoplane	4 hours 10 minutes	Gran had been part of the team that discovered the bodies of Robert Falcon Scott's failed attempt to be the first to reach the South Pole.
Atlantic Ocean (North)	Rockaway Beach, NY, USA to Lisbon, Portugal	8–27 May 1919	Lt Cdr Albert C Read (commander) + five others	Curtis NC-4 flying boat	19 days	The NC flying boats (known as 'Nancies') were designed to be long-range anti-submarine patrol aircraft but arrived too late for the First World War. Three of the four-engined biplanes set off but only one completed the journey.
Atlantic Ocean (South)	Lisbon, Portugal to Rio de Janeiro, Brazil	30 March–17 June 1922	Sacadura Cabral (pilot), Gago Coutinho (navigator)	3 x Fairey F III-D seaplanes (*Lusitania, Pátria, Santa Cruz*)	79 days	The two-man crew were sent two replacement aircraft in order that they complete their objective, hence the long duration of their attempt.
Pacific Ocean	Oakland, CA, USA to Brisbane, Australia	31 May–9 June 1928	Charles Edward Kingsford Smith and Charles Ulm (pilots) + two others	Fokker F.7 *The Southern Cross*	9 days	Distance of 7,938 miles was covered in a three-stage flight.[70]

ONE MILLION

On 1 October 1926 a biplane touched down on the River Thames at Westminster in front of a crowd estimated to be one million strong. The pilot was Alan Cobham and his choice of landing spot was no accident: he landed close to the Houses of Parliament to gain attention for his cause – to see aviation being properly recognised. In a speech he gave not long after, Cobham said: 'We wanted to prove that flying is an everyday affair.'

Cobham's landing was the end of a flight that was by most standards anything but everyday. He was completing the first successful round-trip flight to Australia, a journey of 26,000 miles, flown in his de Havilland DH.50J biplane. Cobham's aircraft had floats instead of a wheeled undercarriage, as it was easier to find water to land on than proper airstrips.

Cobham's outward flight was touched by tragedy as his engineer Arthur Elliott was shot and killed by Bedouins after Cobham was forced to fly lower than normal due to a stand storm. Sergeant Arthur Ward of the RAF took over from Elliot.

B-29 *Fifi* at Oshkosh 2011. (Spartan7W under Creative Commons Licence)

Cobham was knighted for his pioneering flight, the award following the Air Force Cross he was given for the return flight he had completed earlier in the year to South Africa.

Cobham believed that in-flight refuelling was the key to long-distance flight and was a keen proponent of its use, setting up a company called Flight Refuelling Ltd. It developed the probe-and-drogue system used by the RAF and US Navy among others:[71]

ONKEL THEO

Oberst Theo Osterkamp commanded Jagdgeschwader 51 during the Battle of Britain at 48 years of age. He was one of the few pilots to have flown in combat in both the First and Second World Wars. He had shot down thirty-two Allied planes in the First World War and claimed a further six in 1940. Osterkamp's nickname was a sign of affection and respect from the Luftwaffe's pilots. Osterkamp survived the war and died in 1975.[72]

OSHKOSH

What began in 1953 as an informal fly-in featuring forty aircraft is now the world's largest airshow. Organised by the American Experimental Aircraft Association, the week-long event held at Oshkosh, Wisconsin, sees over 10,000 aircraft participating and 500,000 people visiting.

P IS FOR...

PIGGY BACK PLANES

Designers have had to come up with innovative solutions to increase their aircraft's range, whether it be external fuel tanks, aerial refuelling or, another idea used on several occasions that of 'piggy backing': one aircraft on the back of a larger carrier machine. This method was also used to ferry machines that were suited to operating in a different environment.

Maia and *Mercury*

The Short-Mayo composite aircraft consisted of two machines: a Short S.21 flying boat *Maia* (the carrier aircraft) and on top the Short S.20 seaplane *Mercury*. Mayo stemmed from Imperial Airways' technical manager Robert Mayo, who conceived the idea.

The composite was designed to service mail delivery and carry passengers across large distances. With its assisted take off, *Mercury* would then lift off mid flight and carry on its journey alone. The project worked and *Mercury* achieved the first commercial heavier-than-air crossing of the Atlantic in July 1938. It was no rapid crossing – the average speed was 144mph.

In October 1938 *Mercury* flew from Dundee to South Africa. This flight set a new distance record for a seaplane of 6,045 miles, achieved in 42 hours 6 minutes. Both aircraft were destroyed during the Second World War: *Maia* by German bombers; *Mercury* by the need for aluminium.[73]

Mistel

During the Second World War German aircraft designers came up with many unusual concepts. One of the more lethal was that of the Mistel (Mistletoe) which was a combination of an unmanned bomber (a Junkers Ju 88) with its cockpit section filled with explosives, and a guiding fighter aircraft (Messerschmitt Me 109 or Focke-Wulf Fw 190) attached on top. The fighter would fly the two aircraft towards the target and then release

Atlantis on Shuttle Carrier Aircraft. (NASA/Carla Thomas)

the bomber. Some were used against Allied shipping after the D-Day landings and against the Soviet Union's advance in the Eastern Campaign but little success was achieved.[74]

Shuttle Carrier Aircraft

NASA's space shuttle differed from its American manned spaceflight predecessors in that it landed back on dry land rather than in the middle of the ocean. This meant it needed transportation from the landing site at Edwards Air Force Base in California back to the launch site at Cape Kennedy in Florida. With this requirement, two Boeing 747s (N911NA and N905NA) were converted to carry the empty shuttle on their backs. N905NA's last duty was to ferry the shuttles to museums when they were retired from service in 2012.[75]

PIGS CAN FLY

I am the first pig to fly.

The message written on a wicker basket containing a pig flown by British aviator John Moore-Brabazon on 4 November 1909. Moore-Brabazon, who was the first pilot to be awarded his licence in the United Kingdom, had staged the flight to show in a light-hearted manner that with the advent of aviation, pigs could indeed fly.

PILOT'S LICENCE

Neil Armstrong gained his pilot's licence on his sixteenth birthday – 5 August 1946. He had yet to get his driving licence.

PRECISION RAIDS

Modern aerial warfare is dominated by precision strikes and the ability of modern weaponry to be delivered accurately. During the Second World War several precision raids were carried out, among them some notable operations carried out by RAF Mosquitoes. The combination of speed, the weight of bombs able to be carried and range meant it was ideal for low-level raids over occupied Europe.

Target	Location	Date	Unit	No. of Aircraft	Result
Gestapo HQ	Oslo, Norway	25 Sep 1942	105 Squadron	4	Target hit but eighty civilians injured or killed.
Prison	Amiens, France	18 Feb 1944	140 Wing	19	Walls and prison breached, 255 French resistance prisoners escaped though many were recaptured.
Gestapo HQ	The Hague, Netherlands	11 Apr 1944	613 Squadron	6	Target destroyed. Six civilians killed.
SS barracks	Egletons, France	18 Aug 1944	613 Squadron	14	Successful raid, target heavily damaged.
Gestapo HQ	Aarhus, Denmark	31 Oct 1944	140 Wing	25	Target hit successfully.
Gestapo HQ	Shell House, Copenhagen, Denmark	21 Mar 1945	140 Wing	18	Target hit but school bombed in error after Mosquito crashed and 125 killed, including eighty-six children.
Gestapo HQ	Odense, Denmark	17 Apr 1945	140 Wing	6	Target destroyed.[76]

PUÑO AIRLINES

In 1985 passengers arriving at Miami Airport to fly with this airline were surprised when instead of the free flight to the Bahamas and $350 spending money they were expecting, they were arrested by US Marshals. The airline was fictitious and those who had received letters informing them of their great prize were part of a sting. The word 'puño' is Spanish for 'fist'. The arresting officials were part of a Fugitive Investigative Strike Team (FIST).[77]

Q IS FOR...

QF-4

The F-4 Phantom spent much of its lifetime as a fighter whose role was to intercept and shoot down enemy aircraft but the QF-4 variant's job is to be shot down.

Elderly F-4s were retrieved from desert storage 'bone yards' and restored to flying status. At the same time they were equipped to be flown remotely from the ground as Full-Scale Aerial Targets. The aircraft can also be flown by pilots and some of the QF-4s were used to display at US airshows.

Other aircraft have operated in this role such as the QF-102 Delta Dagger, QF-100 Super Sabre, and QF-106 Delta Dart. The QF-4s will be replaced by another famous fighter, with F-16s becoming QF-16s.[78]

QRA

Britain's Royal Air Force maintains a 24-hour, 7-day-a-week system of home defence based on Quick Reaction Alert (QRA). Eurofighter Typhoon fighters based at Lossiemouth in Moray and Coningsby in Lincolnshire are kept armed and fuelled with pilots standing by ready to take off when directed by the fighter controllers who detect any untoward aircraft approaching the United Kingdom.

This QRA system has been in force since the Cold War utilising Lightnings, Phantoms and Tornado F.3s, before the introduction of the Typhoon. Aircraft would quickly launch and intercept targets, which were often Soviet, aircraft flying close to the UK's airspace.One Phantom pilot was Robert Prest who flew with 43 Squadron at RAF Leuchars during the 1970s. He wrote a much-regarded book about his experiences, which remains a fascinating insight into RAF fighter operations during this period, which was normally cloaked behind secrecy. In his book *F-4 Phantom – A Pilot's Story* he describes a night-time flight when he was sent on patrol northwards from Scotland towards the Arctic Circle:

> A blip materialises on my radar screen. An electronic pulse has seized on the metal, plucking it from the darkness. We report it. The controller admits he is baffled. It does not figure in any published flight plan. It is not sending out a recognisable identification. He instructs us to investigate. We all know what it probably is – some airliner off course, straying away from the beaten airways track, maybe a fault in its inertial system or a couple of degrees' error in heading undetected by the crew. We don't care; it is there and it is something to do to stop us dozing off in the soporific atmosphere – all quiet on the Northern front – we home towards the contact and carry out a standard vis-ident approach, stealing up from low in the stern. As we turn in, I look out, eyes straining to penetrate the blackness. There is a patch of sky that is uncharacteristically devoid of stars, a patch that is nevertheless shifting slowly. We close in the turn, and suddenly we can see the rows

of lighted portholes running along the sides of the patch. We delay our report for a while and close right up beneath the shape. At this range, it spreads hugely, blanking out half the Milky Way Galaxy. Four long, wispy condensation trails steam from the great engines, the wing tip navigation lights spread from horizon to horizon. It sits solidly, effortlessly, a colossus apparently unmoving, Juggernaut in the Sky. It is a 747 Jumbo, possibly en route to the States from Tokyo via the Polar route? Who knows … who cares? We sit and admire its massiveness for a while and I smile as I imagine the bustling humanity existing inside, sleeping, eating, drinking, watching the in-flight movies, trim hostesses tramping the aisles with their trays. I think of the flight crew sitting quietly bored atop that great fuselage, making their airways report, filling in the flight log; a moving microcosm of humanity, a city in the sky, and all blissfully unaware of the Black Widow, the Black Mamba, the Black Panther, the Tiger Shark lurking a few feet away in the darkness behind watching silently with glowing eyes, evil dealer of death and destruction, alien war machine …

From *F4 Phantom: A Pilot's Story* by Robert Prest (Corgi, 1981) with kind permission of the author.

QUIET BIRDMEN

The bearer is a member of ye Ancient and Secret Order of Quiet Birdmen founded January 1921 and is a certified goodfellow. He has mounted alone into the realms beyond the reach of Keewee and Modock and should be accorded all gestures of friendship and aid by fellow Quiet Birdmen wherever they may meet.

This is the inscription on the membership cards of a private group of fliers, who meet regularly in separate 'Hangars'. Founded in 1921, the Quiet Birdmen keep the location of meetings and membership a closely guarded secret, although one meeting in September 1941 was not quite so covert. It was held to honour those who had taken part in the Battle of Britain. Among those who attended this London 'Hangar' were distinguished guests such as:

- Air Chief Marshal Hugh Dowding
- Air Marshal Trafford Leigh-Mallory
- Brigadier General James Doolittle
- Group Captain Basil Embry
- Lt General Dwight D. Eisenhower

- Major General Carl Spaatz
- Squadron Leader Johnnie Johnson
- Wing Commander 'Sailor' Malan
- Wing Commander Brian Kingcome
- Wing Commander Johnny Kent
- Wing Commander Max Aitken
- Wing Commander Ian Gleed[79]

QUIMBY, HARRIET

Harriet Quimby achieved many notable firsts in aviation, being the first woman in America to gain a pilot's licence and the first woman to fly an aircraft at night. However it was her achievement on 16 April 1912 that gained her widespread fame when she became the first woman to pilot an aircraft over the English Channel. Her flight in a Bleriot XI monoplane saw her being named 'America's First Lady of the Air'. Quimby died on 1 July 1912 during an air meet at Boston after being thrown clear of her aircraft as she flew over Dorchester Bay. She had said before taking off: 'I have no intention of coming down in the water.'[80]

QUOTATIONS

I have not the smallest molecule of faith in aerial navigation other than ballooning.[81]

Lord Kelvin, scientist.

It is easy to invent a flying machine; more difficult to build one. To make it fly is everything.[82]

Otto Lillenthal, glider pioneer.

Every flying field I have known is soaked with the blood of my friends and brother pilots. My memory is one long obituary list.[83]

Anton Fokker, aircraft designer.

Higher, always higher.

Jorge Chávez.

The last words of Peruvian pioneer aviator Jorge Chávez who died following the first successful flight over the Alps, on 23 September 1910. Chávez's words continue to serve as inspiration to modern day aviation in his country.[84]

That Wilbur Wright is in possession of a power, which controls the fate of nations, is beyond dispute.[85]

>   Major B.F.S. Baden-Powell, President of
>   the Royal Aeronautical Society.

Baden-Powell was flown by Wilbur Wright during his visit to Europe in 1908.

We are beaten![86]

>   French aviator Leon Delagrange after seeing Wilbur Wright's
>   flying demonstrations in France in 1908.

The time will come when flying will be the ordinary means of rapid locomotion all over the world for long distances.[87]

>   Charles C. Turner, aviator and author in 1912.

When death comes to me, I should like it to be … sharp and sudden. Death in one of my own aeroplanes.

>   Samuel F. Cody.

Cody died when his own aircraft crashed in August 1913.[88]

Once we got the Mach jump on the Mach meter – and all the buffeting smoothed out it was almost a let-down – the damned thing didn't blow up![89]

>   Charles 'Chuck' Yeager on his historic flight in October 1947 that saw
>   an aircraft fly faster than the speed of sound for the first time.

Aviation is fine as a sport, but as an instrument of war, it is worthless.[90]

>   French General Ferdinand Foch, March 1913.

This flying is the most wonderful invention. A man ceases to be human up there. He feels that nothing is impossible.[91]

>   Canadian fighter pilot Billy Bishop, 1915.

I hope he roasted all the way down.

>   Royal Flying Corps fighter ace Edward 'Mick' Mannock on hearing
>   of the death of Manfred von Richthofen.

When he was an ace von Richthofen had shot down 80 Allied aircraft in April 1918.

We're down, lads.[92]

> Chief Coxswain G. W. Hunt to crew of airship R.101 moments
> before it crashed. Hunt died in the accident.

I do not believe in safety first because I do not think it gets us anywhere; but
I do believe in taking every precaution you can and then taking risks.[93]

> Amy Johnson, August 1930, after her
> return from Australia.

It is improbable that any terrorization of the civil population, which could
be achieved by air attack, would compel the Government of a great nation
to surrender.[94]

> Winston Churchill, Minister of Munitions, October 1917.

Anton Fokker.
(Library of
Congress, Prints
& Photographs
Division, LC-B2-
5258-7)

There are a lot of people who say that bombing can never win a war. Well, my answer to that is that it has never been tried yet, and we shall see.

RAF Air Marshal Arthur 'Bomber' Harris, 1942.

The airplane was completely under control right up to the time it hit the house.[95]
Howard Hughes, on the crash of the XF-11 in 1946.

I will fly the cockpit and I imagine the rest of the aeroplane will follow me.
Bristol Brabazon test pilot Bill Pegg before the giant aircraft's first flight in 1949.

We had a terrible journey. The wonder is we are here at all.[96]
John Alcock, following the epic transatlantic flight.

And when that time comes that I can no longer be written to, people will not set off on voyages of discovery in the Arctic regions any more. Then, air routes will follow the great circles, unaffected by the Arctic.[97]
Hjalmar Riiser-Larsen, Norwegian aviation pioneer, who had been Roald Amundsen's pilot on his 1925 North Pole expedition.

R IS FOR...

RECORD FLIGHT

Aviation lent itself to those pilots wishing to go faster, or higher, or further than anyone else. Records were being set from the very beginning and the pace of advance was so fast that by the 1950s the records being established would have appeared incredible to those early flyers.

On 7 May 1958, Major Howard J. 'Scrappy' Johnson of the US Air Force took off in a Lockheed F-104A Starfighter with the intention of breaking the aircraft altitude record that stood at 76,932ft, set by a US Navy Grumman Super Tiger less than a month before. Johnson's flight ran as follows:

Milestone	Details
Take-off	Airfield: Palmdale, California.
Transit	To Santa Barbara, to turn and begin run towards Edwards Air Force Base.

43,000ft	With aircraft at optimum altitude, afterburner selected and aircraft accelerates.
Mach 2.23	Once reached, aircraft pulls into a 52° climb.
63,000ft	Afterburner stops working due to lack of air.
67,000ft	Engine stops working due to lack of air. Aircraft continues to climb ballistically.
91,243ft	Aircraft reaches maximum height. (Speed is at 30 knots).
Descent	At 47,000ft engine is restarted.
Landing	Safely achieved at Palmdale.[98]

RED ARROWS REMEMBRANCE

Since their formation in 1965 the Red Arrows have been the RAF's premier aerobatic display team. They have flown over 4,000 displays, firstly in Folland Gnats and currently BAE Systems Hawks. Ten pilots have lost their lives flying with the team:

1969	Flight Lieutenant Jerry Bowler
1971	Flight Lieutenant Euan Perreaux, Flight Lieutenant John Lewis, Flight Lieutenant John Haddock, Flight Lieutenant Colin Armstrong
1978	Flight Lieutenant Stephen Noble, Wing Commander Dennis Hazell
1988	Flight Lieutenant Neil MacLachlan
2011	Flight Lieutenant Jon Egging, Flight Lieutenant Sean Cunningham

REGINALD A.J. WARNEFORD

The First World War saw several weapons being introduced, such as the armoured tank, long-range submarines and combat aircraft. Another innovation was long-range strategic bombing. The British eventually developed aircraft to bomb targets in Germany but it was the Germans who made advantage of their technological lead in airship designs: Zeppelins had begun bombing the United Kingdom in January 1915.

They roamed mostly untroubled by Allied air forces until the night of 6/7 June 1915 when Flight Sub-Lieutenant Reginald A.J. Warneford of the Royal Naval Air Service spotted LZ.37 near the coast of Belgium. In his Morane-Saulnier Parasol he flew above the airship and dropped six bombs. His target exploded and fell to the ground near Ghent. Warneford's aircraft was thrown upside down by the blast and its engine was stopped. He made a forced landing behind enemy lines, but was able to restart and take off. Within 24 hours he was awarded the Victoria Cross, but died ten days afterwards in a flying accident.

REIMS

The world's first large-scale international airshow – or *Grande Semaine d'Aviation de la Champagne* – was held at Reims in France between 22 and 29 August 1909.

The event featured participants such as Louis Bleriot, who had recently completed the first crossing of the English Channel; Henri Farman; Hubert Latham (who had failed to beat Bleriot); and American Glenn Curtiss who along with Scotsman George Cockburn were the only non-French fliers from the twenty-two who took part. Bleriot's aircraft was lost in a crash on the last day.

The main event was the contest for the Gordon Bennett Aviation Trophy, one of six for heavier-than-air machines. There was also a dirigible speed and a balloon landing prize.

The aircraft events were:

Event	Details	Winner's Prize	Winner	Results
Circuit Prize	Fastest circuit attained	7,000 francs	Louis Bleriot	7 min 47 sec
Gordon Bennett Aviation Trophy	Two circuits of a 10km course in the shortest time	£1,000 and his aero club received £500.	Glenn Curtiss	15 min 50 sec
Grand Prix of Champagne and the City of Reims	Longest distance flight	50,000 francs	Henri Farman	112 miles
Height Prize	Greatest altitude gained	10,000 francs	Hubert Latham	508ft[99]
Passengers' Prize	Entrant that carried the most passengers on one circuit	10,000 francs	Henri Farman	Two passengers
Speed Prize	Fastest over three circuits of the course	10,000 francs	Glenn Curtiss	23min 29 sec

It is estimated that up to half a million people watched the event during the week, showing the intense interest in aviation at this time.

RHODES-MOORHOUSE

Tomorrow I am going out at a very early hour, long, long before you will be out of bed, on an expedition, which, if this letter reaches home, I shall be dead.

Part of a letter from Royal Flying Corps pilot William Rhodes-Moorhouse to William, his 1-year-old son. On 26 April 1915 Rhodes-Moorhouse flew on a solo-bombing raid on the railway yards at Courtrai, which was a hub for German troops being moved to the front to take part in the Battle of Ypres. His biplane was hit many times as he flew at low-level and he was severely injured. Despite this he was able to fly back to his airfield at Merville where he insisted on giving his report. He died of his wounds the next day. Rhodes-Moorhouse was the first Royal Flying Corps airman to be awarded the Victoria Cross.

The wreckage of Bleriot's aircraft. (Library of Congress, Prints & Photographs Division, LC-USZ62-94562)

The recipient of his letter, his son, joined the RAF and flew from the same airfield as his father during the Battle of France in 1940. He was killed during the Battle of Britain in September that year.[100]

ROBERT WATSON-WATT

It is, I believe, agreed that so far as concerns material, the first Battle of Britain was won by radar and the 8-gun fighter.

Robert Watson-Watt, in a letter to Archibald Sinclair, Secretary of State for Air, 21 December 1940. Watson-Watt developed a system of detecting aircraft by radio waves and capturing their position and height. It formed the basis for Britain's 'Chain Home' radar installations that were instrumental in the Battle of Britain.

ROLLING

On 7 August 1955 Boeing test pilot Alvin 'Tex' Johnson was asked to demonstrate his company's new prototype airliner – the four-engined Dash 80. Johnson did so, but in a way that no one expected. After carrying out a pass in front of a watching crowd of 200,000 he returned and then applied full aileron, taking the big jet into a complete 360-degree roll. To make sure everyone who saw it could believe his or her eyes he repeated the manoeuvre. The following day he was invited to a meeting with the chairman of Boeing who told him not to do it again.

Although rare, Johnson's roll was not unique amongst pilots flying large aircraft. The same year, Roly Falk rolled the Avro Vulcan V-bomber at the Farnborough air show. In 1988 Concorde pilot Brian Walpole described how he and French test pilot Jean Franchi both took the controls to barrel roll the supersonic airliner jet.

RUHR DAMS RAID

Two of the dams are known to be breached and the other damaged. Water is seen pouring through a great gap in the Moehne Dam and widespread damage has been caused by the rush of water down the valley. Two villages are seen flooded, bridges swept away, power stations and water works isolated and railway communications disrupted. Although the Eder dam is not covered on these photographs there is evidence of damage caused by floods on a similar scale and over an ever wider area than in the Moehne valley.

Immediate Interpretation Report No K.1559, 18 May 1943.

This was the initial report following three RAF photographic reconnaissance missions flown on 18 May, the day after 617 Squadron attacked the Ruhr dams. The Dambusters had flown at ultra low-level (60ft) and dropped a specially designed 'bouncing bomb'. The Moehne and Eder dams were breached and although the raid was deemed a success in terms of its aims, almost half the attacking Lancasters didn't return. An estimated 1,600 German civilians and Allied prisoners-of-war were killed. The bombing of dams was later outlawed under the Geneva Conventions.[101]

S IS FOR...

SABRE DANCE

American F-100 Super Sabre fighters were prone to severe control issues when at slow speed. With the nose high at increased angles of attack, as the F-100 slowed towards stalling speed, the centre of lift moved forward and the aircraft pitched up. This led to adverse yaw, which had to be controlled by the rudders, not the wings' ailerons, as they were ineffective due to the wingtips stalling before the rest of the wing – a problem of the Super Sabre's 45-degree swept-wing design.

On 10 January 1956 Lieutenant Barty R. Brooks achieved a grim type of fame when he was filmed attempting to land at Edwards Air Force Base with a Sabre that had a nose-wheel undercarriage problem. In order to lengthen his landing run he pulled the nose up, slowing the aircraft down and beginning what became known as the 'Sabre Dance'. The film of him trying to apply afterburner to increase speed but eventually losing control and crashing was used as a training film.[102]

SALOMON AUGUST ANDRÉE

Andrée was a Swedish aeronaut who was determined to be the first to cross the Arctic in a balloon. On 11 July 1897 along with two other

Swedes Knut Frænkel and Nils Strindberg, he took off from Spitsbergen in hydrogen balloon *The Eagle*. Carrier pigeons had been taken and the last one to be sent had the message: 'July 13, 12.30pm. Latitude 82, longitude 15 east; good speed towards east, 10 degrees south. All well on board. This is the third pigeon post. Andrée.'

No more communications were received, and it took thirty-three years to discover what had happened. A Norwegian ship visited White Island, the most easterly part of the Svalbard archipelago, and found the bodies of the three men. Along with the bodies journals and photographic film were found. It transpired that their attempt was doomed from the start. Soon after take off they were in danger of landing in the sea so had dumped a lot of ballast. This meant they rose up too high and lost more hydrogen than they could afford. The balloon then accumulated ice and was unable to fly properly and bumped along the ground. After a few days it came to Earth for good and the three men began a survival attempt. They had much in the way of supplies when they started walking across the rugged terrain. They ended up drifting on ice floes and when the floes started to break up they landed on White Island. It is thought they died not long after reaching the island. One appeared to have died of a polar bear attack.

The return of their bodies saw national mourning. The Swedish king, Gustav V said: 'In the name of the Swedish nation, I here greet the dust of the polar explorers who, more than three decades ago, left their native land to find an answer to questions of unparalleled difficulty.'[103]

SAMS

The widespread deployment of Surface-to-Air Missiles (SAMs) during the Cold War changed the face of military aircraft operations. This was highlighted when an American U-2 spy plane was shot down by a SA-2 Guideline missile in May 1960 and its pilot Francis Gary Powers was captured, put on trial for spying and jailed. In the Vietnam War the North Vietnamese used Soviet-built SAMs extensively and new electronic counter-measures had to be brought in. High altitude bombing raids were no longer possible in the way seen in the Second World War: attacking strike aircraft now had to fly low-level to escape the radar-directed SAMs. The development of highly portable shoulder-launched missiles such as Blowpipe and Stinger brought another factor to be considered and counter measures such as flares were developed.

Cold War SAMs

UK
Bloodhound
Blowpipe
Rapier
Sea Cat
Sea Dart
Sea Slug
Sea Wolf
Thunderbird

USA
Bomarc
Hawk

Nike Ajax
Nike Hercules
Redeye
Stinger

USSR *
SA-1 Guild
SA-2 Guideline
SA-3 Goa
SA-4 Ganef
SA-5 Gammon
SA-6 Gainful
SA-7 Grail

SA-8 Gecko
SA-9 Gaskin
SA-10 Grumble
SA-11 Gadfly
SA-12 Gladiator/Giant
SA-13 Gopher
SA-14 Gremlin
SA-15 Gauntlet
SA-16 Gimlet
SA-17 Grizzly
SA-18 Grouse
SA-19 Grison

*NATO reporting names used

SANDY

When one of their aircraft is brought down in combat the United States Air Force (USAF) sends rescue aircraft on what are called 'Sandy' missions. The name comes from a USAF pilot who first used the word as a call sign when flying such missions in Vietnam. Sandy was the name of his pet dog.[104]

SCHNEIDER TROPHY

A French businessman who wished to promote the development of seaplanes in Europe set up the Schneider Trophy competition. The event, officially the *Coupe d'Aviation Maritime Jacques Schneider*, was won by the fastest aircraft over a set distance. The winning nation hosted the next race. What began as a race amongst private entries turned into a competition between nations, at times using their professional air force pilots and ground crews, investing large sums to compete properly.

Year	Location	Winning Nation	Aircraft	Average Speed (mph)	Notes
1913	Monaco, France	France	Deperdussin monoplane	46	Four contestants.
1914	Monaco, France	UK	Sopwith Tabloid	87	Nine contestants.

1919	Bournemouth, UK	No winner	-	-	Event was cancelled due to fog but despite this Italy flew fastest lap.
1920	Venice, Italy	Italy	Savoia S.12	107	Italy was only country that entered.
1921	Venice, Italy	Italy	Macchi M.7bis	117	Italy again was the sole country competing after French aircraft failed to take off.
1922	Naples, Italy	UK	Supermarine Sea Lion II	146	Britain's first victory (with aircraft designed by R.J. Mitchell, the future Spitfire designer) prevented Italy from achieving three consecutive victories – and thus retaining the trophy.
1923	Cowes, Isle of Wight, UK	USA	Curtiss CR-3	177	America's first appearance.
1924	Baltimore, USA	No winner	-	-	British entry crashed in trials. Italy and France had withdrawn. America who would win unopposed, sportingly cancelled the event.
1925	Baltimore, USA	USA	Curtis R3C-2	233	Winning pilot was Lieutenant James H. Doolittle.
1926	Norfolk, Virginia, USA	Italy	Macchi M.39	248	Winning engine was rated at 800hp – four times that of the winner only five years previously.
1927	Venice, Italy	UK	Supermarine S.5	282	S.5s finished first and second.
1929	Cowes, Isle of Wight, UK	UK	Supermarine S.6	329	Rolls-Royce provided the Supermarine's engine. Italy was only other nation competing.
1931	Cowes, Isle of Wight, UK	UK	Supermarine S.6B	340	Italy, France and USA did not sent entries and Britain chose to continue, thus retaining the trophy.[105]

SHAMBLES

It was the finest shambles I have been in since for once we had position, height and numbers. Enemy aircraft were a dirty looking collection.

Squadron Leader Douglas Bader, commander 242 Squadron, combat report for 15 September 1940, the day when the RAF resistance to the

Luftwaffe's daylight bombing campaign proved a critical turning point in the Battle of Britain.

SKYTRAIN

Launched in September 1977 Skytrain was the first low-cost transatlantic service, instigated by airline entrepreneur Freddie Laker. Tickets to New York from London, Gatwick Airport cost £59 – a third that of the main rivals – and passengers didn't book in advance but bought their tickets at the airport and flew on the next available flight. It was a 'no-frills' service, with passengers having to buy any food on the flight. Laker's innovation was a huge success but the rival operators forced him out of business and Laker Airways went into receivership in 1982. Laker later won a court case and received compensation.

SONGS ABOUT AVIATION

Song	Singer/Group
747 (Strangers in the Night)	Saxon
Airport	The Motors
Bomber	Motörhead
Come Fly With Me	Frank Sinatra
Enola Gay	OMD
Jet Airliner	Steve Miller Band
Learn to Fly	Foo Fighters
Leaving on a Jet Plane	John Denver
Spitfire	Public Service Broadcasting
This Flight Tonight	Joni Mitchell

SPITFIRE GIFTS

Vickers-Supermarine's Spitfire caught the imagination of the public almost as soon as it came out of the factory in the 1930s. Its hold as an icon of British aviation remains and its image and shape have been used in numerous items available to buy:

Prints, cufflinks, postcards, beer, built models, mounted control columns, biscuit tins, plastic model kits, ceramic plates, mugs, cushions, T-shirts, mouse mats, watches, birthday cards, caps, key rings, jam jar spoons, socks, key chains, pens, laser-etched crystal cubes, jigsaws, clocks, calendars, hip flasks, wine glasses, mustard, lap trays, tie pins, spectacle cases, phone cases, lens cleaning cloths, wallpaper, bookmarks, tie racks, guitar picks, cigarette lighters, coasters, notepads, weekly planners, coin sets, shoulder bags, money clips, fridge magnets, pillows, bottle openers, medallions.

SPITFIRE QUOTES

The Spitfire attracted much praise for its looks and flying qualities from those who flew it in the Second World War.

She was really the perfect flying machine.[106]

Flight Sergeant George Unwin.

It was a delight to fly.[107]

Pilot Officer James Goodson.

She was such a gentle little aeroplane, without a trace of viciousness. She was a dream to handle in the air.[108]

2nd Lieutenant Ervin Miller, USAAF.

It is so small and compact and neat, yet it possesses devastating fire power.[109]

Flight Lieutenant David Crook.

I consider it to have been the best operational fighter of them all.[110]

Flight Lieutenant Ian Ponsford.

The most beautiful and finest aeroplane in the world … it was a superb fighting aeroplane and it was pilot's dream.[111]

Squadron Leader Raymond Baxter.

She was a true thoroughbred.[112]

Wing Commander Robert Stanford-Tuck.

An incomparable fighting machine but also indefinably at the same time a thing of sheer beauty.[113]

Flight Lieutenant Richard Gilman.

The prettiest things ever built.

Group Captain Douglas Bader.

Spitfire. (Norman Ferguson)

The Spitfire is the most beautiful aeroplane that's ever been made.[114]

Wing Commander Robert 'Bob' Doe.

A magnificent aeroplane...[115]

Squadron Leader Geoffrey Wellum.

It was a wonderful thing.[116]

Pilot Officer Tom Neil.

STATUES

There are numerous memorials and statues of aviation figures and events. Many come in the shape of wall plaques and there are more unusual ones such as the Frank Whittle Roundabout in Lutterworth, Leicestershire, which features a replica Gloster E.28/39, the first jet aircraft to fly in the United Kingdom. Among the UK's statues are these:[117]

Subject	Location	Year unveiled
Charles Rolls	Monmouth	1911
Albert Ball VC	Nottingham Castle	1921
Alcock and Brown	Heathrow Airport	1954
Amy Johnson	Hull	1974
ACM Hugh Dowding	London	1988
Douglas Bader	Goodwood (ex-RAF Westhampnett)	2001
Sir Frank Whittle	Coventry	2007
AVM Keith Park	London	2010
Samuel F. Cody	Farnborough	2013
Robert Watson-Watt	Brechin	2014

T IS FOR...

TELEVISION

Aviation-related drama series have not been as numerous as movie releases but nonetheless some notable programmes have been made:

Title	Country	Broadcast	Details
Whirlybirds	USA	1957–60	111 episodes were made about the adventures of two Bell 47 pilots, who ran a helicopter-for-hire company.
The Plane Makers	UK	1963–65	An aircraft manufacturing company and its ruthless managing director was the subject of this ITV series.
Les chevaliers du ciel (The Knights of the Sky)	France	1967–70	Series about two French fighter pilots flying Mirage III jets. Was dubbed into English and shown in UK as *The Aeronauts*.
Wings	UK	1977–78	The experiences of pilots in a Royal Flying Corps squadron on the Western Front featured in two series of this BBC drama.

Buccaneer	UK	1980	This series about fictional freight carrier Redair only ran for one series as the aircraft that featured, a Bristol Britannia, was lost in a fatal crash.
Airline	UK	1982	Only one series was made of this story about a man, played by Roy Marsden, setting up a civilian airline in post-Second World War Britain.
Squadron	UK	1982	A BBC series featuring the RAF's fictional 370 Rapid Deployment Squadron.
Airwolf	USA	1984–87	Test pilot Stringfellow Hawke flew the eponymous advanced helicopter in adventures against forces of evil in an attempt to have the government find his brother, posted missing in Vietnam.
The Flying Doctors	Australia	1986–92	Long-running series on the Royal Flying Doctor Service, flying from the outback town of Cooper's Crossing.
Piece of Cake	UK	1988	A RAF fighter squadron in the Battle of Britain based on the Derek Robinson novel.

TEST FLIGHT REPORT

Test Flight Report No:	1
Type of test:	1st flight.
Date and Time of Start:	15 May 1941, 1940 hours
Duration:	17 minutes
Aircraft (Type and Number):	E.28/39 W4041
Airscrew (Type and Number):	No airscrew fitted with this method of propulsion.

This last entry in a test flight form signalled the start of a new era in British aviation. The test pilot who filled in the form was Flight Lieutenant Jerry Sayer, who that day successfully flew the Gloster E.28/39 – Britain's first jet aircraft. The aircraft (nicknamed 'Squirt') was powered by an engine designed by Frank Whittle.[118]

TEST PILOT MEMOIRS

Test flying has always been a dangerous occupation and those who survived have shown a blend of skill and luck. Those that have been able to record their experiences in book form include:

- Alex Henshaw – *Sigh for a Merlin. Testing the Spitfire*
- Bill Waterton – *The Quick and the Dead. The Perils of Post-War Test Flying*
- Eric 'Winkle' Brown – *Wings on my Sleeve*
- Jeffrey Quill – *Spitfire: A Test Pilot's Story*
- John Farley – *A View from the Hover. My Life in Aviation.*
- Mike Brooke – *Trials and Errors: Experimental UK Test Flying in the 1970s*
- Neville Duke – *Test Pilot*
- Peter Twiss – *Faster Than the Sun: The Compelling Story of a Record-breaking Test Pilot and WWII Navy Flyer*
- Roland 'Bee' Beamont – *The Years Flew Past: 40 Years at the Leading Edge of Aviation*
- Tony Blackman – *Vulcan Test Pilot. My Experiences in the Cockpit of a Cold War Icon*

TICKER TAPE PARADES

New York has a tradition of honouring notable figures and their achievements with 'ticker tape' parades through downtown New York, where those being honoured are showered with paper from the surrounding skyscrapers. Aviators (excluding those who were honoured for their exploits in space) have featured strongly in the parades:

Year	Date	Names	Details
1926	23 June	Commander Richard E. Byrd and Floyd Bennett	First flight to North Pole.
1927	13 June	Charles Lindbergh	First solo flight over Atlantic.
	18 July	Commander Richard E. Byrd and crew of *America*, jointly held with Clarence Chamberlin	Two transatlantic flights.
	11 November	Ruth Elder and George W. Haldeman	First woman to attempt transatlantic flight.
1928	30 April	Captain Hermann Köhl, Major Fitzmaurice and Baron von Hünefeld	First east-west aircraft crossing of Atlantic.
	6 July	Amelia Earhart, Wilmer Stultz, Lou Gordon	First woman to fly the Atlantic.
	16 October	Crew of *Graf Zeppelin*	First commercial flight across Atlantic.

1929	30 August	Crew of *Graf Zeppelin*	First round-the-world airship flight.
1930	19 June	Rear Admiral Richard E. Byrd and members of expedition	Flight over South Pole.
	4 September	Dieudonné Costes and Maurice Bellonte	First non-stop heavier-than air flight from Paris to New York.
1931	2 July	Wiley Post, Harold Gatty	Around-the-world flight record.
1932	20 June	Amelia Earhart	First woman to fly solo across the Atlantic.
1933	21 July	Italo Balbo and crews	First formation crossing of the Atlantic.
	26 July	Wiley Post	First solo around-the-world flight.
	1 August	Amy Johnson and James Mollison	Flight from Wales to Connecticut.
1938	15 July	Howard Hughes	Round-the-world flight record.
	5 August	'Wrong Way' Corrigan	Flew from New York to Ireland, instead of to California.
1946	25 October	Colonel Clarence S. Irvine and crew	B-29 flight from Hawaii to Cairo over North Pole.[119]

TIP AND RUN

'Tip and run' was the term given to raids by Luftwaffe aircraft on Britain's south coast, beginning in 1941. Aircraft such as Messerschmitt Me 109s would fly low-level across the English Channel to evade detection and then make quick attacks on targets such as shipping, ports, gas-works and so on. They were difficult to counter by the means that had played such an important role in the Battle of Britain: radar coverage and Observer Corps visual sightings providing location information for RAF fighters. By the time the system had relayed the information, the raiders had turned for their bases.

Two code-named methods of improving raid detection were brought in:

Totter

Observer Posts, with Coastguard stations, were given pyrotechnic rockets, which were to be fired as soon as raiders were spotted and continued to be launched while the raiders were close by. This would alert the position to standing patrols of RAF fighters.

Rats

This was a code word to begin any sighting report by Observer Corps personnel, which would speed up the process of vectoring defensive fighters to the Observer Corps' position.[120]

TORNADO F.3 DISPLAY

The Panavia Tornado was designed as a multi-role combat aircraft able to carry out reconnaissance, ground-attack and nuclear strike missions. It was adapted into a fighter, with a lengthened nose to accommodate a different type of radar and some other changes. This was the F.3 mark. They were not agile dogfighters in comparison to their counterparts like the American F-15 or Soviet Union's Sukhoi Su 27 but were particularly fast at low-level, something that was shown during their airshow display routines.

In 1993 the display routine, flown by Flight Lieutenants Jerry Goatham and Paul Brown of 56 (R) Squadron was as follows:

Tornado F.3 taking off at 2010 RAF Leuchars Airshow. (Norman Ferguson)

- Take off (or low approach as for landing).
- Climbing turn, 170 knots.
- Minimum Radius Turn, 240 knots, pulling 4g.
- Pull-up into Derry Turn, 290 knots, pulling 4.5g.
- Inverted Pass, 320 knots.
- Pull-up into Half Cuban 8 (5,000ft), 320 knots, pulling 4.5g.
- Canadian Break into Maximum Rate Turn, 330 knots, pulling 5.5–6g.
- Derry Turn, 360 knots.
- Slow Roll, 360 knots.
- Derry Turn (hesitation).
- Slow 'dirty' pass (wheels down, wings swept back), 220 knots.
- Pull-up to Half Horizontal 8 (4,500ft), 250 knots.
- 270° turn (ending towards crowd), 330 knots.
- Pull-up to vertical into Quarter Clover (5,000ft), 320 knots pulling 5.5g.
- Derry Turn (hesitation).
- 4-point Hesitation Roll, 400 knots.
- Derry Turn (wing-over), 450 knots.
- Fast Pass (100ft), 600 knots.
- Pull-up to Vertical, pulling 7g.
- Descent from 24,000ft to land.[121]

TRAGEDY

On 25 September 1958 the press were invited aboard the aircraft carrier HMS *Victorious* to witness the arrival of the Fleet Air Arm's new jet aircraft, the Supermarine Scimitar, as it deployed offshore for the first time. The first aircraft that landed was flown by 803 Squadron's commanding officer, Commander J.D. Russell. He successfully caught the arrestor wire but as he slowed, the wire snapped and his jet slowly continued towards the side of the deck. It rolled over the side and fell into the water. Despite urgent attempts by Commander Russell and a winchman lowered by Whirlwind helicopter, he was unable to be freed from the cockpit and drowned as his jet sank. At one point the canopy was opened a little but it slid closed. The tragedy was made worse by it being filmed and later broadcast. His body was recovered a month later.[122]

TRAPPED

> Hello, I'm stuck in this plane … I'm inside a plane. I feel like it's moving in the air. Flight 448. Can you please tell somebody to stop it?

This phone call was made by a baggage handler who fell asleep inside the cargo hold of an Alaska Airlines aircraft on 13 April 2015. The man's desperate call to 911 resulted in the Boeing 737 aircraft turning round and landing back at Seattle-Tacoma International Airport where it had taken off 22 minutes before. His colleagues had noticed him missing but presumed he'd already left work for the day. Employed by Menzies Aviation, he was later banned by Alaska Airlines from working on any of their future flights.[123]

TRILLION

In 2015 the US government estimated that its newest military aircraft would cost around $1 trillion to operate over its planned lifetime. In addition, to buy the Lockheed Martin F-35 aircraft would cost nearly $400 billion, making it the US government's most expensive military project. The USA plans to buy 2,457 of the aircraft, the first of which entered service in July 2015 with the US Marine Corps. Highly publicised issues over reliability, software and doubts over performance delayed the development of the aircraft, named Lightning II. During a test dogfight with the earlier F-16 fighter, there were moments when the F-35 pilot was unable to see his opponent due to the design of his helmet. The stealthy high technology machine is due to enter service with the United Kingdom, Israel, Japan, South Korea, Italy, the Netherlands, Turkey, Canada, Australia, Denmark and Norway.[124]

TRUCULENT TURTLE

The *Truculent Turtle* was a Lockheed P2V Neptune that set a world record for long-distance flight. On 29 September 1946 it took off from Perth in Australia and set off across the Pacific. Fifty-five hours (and 17 minutes) later it landed in Columbus, Ohio, after flying 11,235 miles non-stop. It had flown this distance without being refuelled. Its record remained in place until beaten by the eight-engined B-52 in 1962.[125]

TWENTY-TWO

The RAF's 'Black Arrows' aerobatic team famously looped with twenty-two Hawker Hunter aircraft at the 1958 Farnborough airshow, creating a world record that still stands.

U IS FOR...

UK AIR DISASTERS

The ten worst air disasters in the UK.

Fatalities	Survivors	Year	Airline	Aircraft	Details
270	0	1988	Pan Am	Boeing 747 N739PA *Clipper Maid of the Seas*	A bomb exploding in a cargo bay caused catastrophic structural damage to the aircraft which fell to the ground, sections of which landed on the Scottish town of Lockerbie, killing eleven residents.
118	0	1972	British European Airways	Trident G-ARPI	Aircraft stalled and it crashed near Staines, 2½ minutes after taking off from Heathrow.
80	3	1950	Airflight Limited	Avro Tudor V G-AKBY *Star Girl*	Welsh rugby fans were returning from their team's victory in Ireland when the aircraft stalled on approach to landing at Llandow. At the time it was the world's worst air crash.
72	12	1967	British Midland Airways	Canadair C-4 Argonaut G-ALHG	Due to fuel starvation, the aircraft lost power from two engines on its approach to land at Ringway Airport and crashed in the town of Stockport.
55	82	1985	British Airtours	Boeing 737 G-BGJL *River Orrin*	The aircraft was consumed by fire after an abandoned take off at Manchester Airport.

50	14	1969	Ariana Afghan Airlines	Boeing 727 YA-FAR	Pilot error caused it to impact the ground while landing at London's Gatwick Airport.
47	79	1989	British Midland	Boeing 737 G-OBME	On approach to East Midlands airport a failing engine ceased working and the aircraft impacted the ground beside a motorway near Kegworth.
45	2	1986	British International Helicopters	Boeing Vertol 234 LR Chinook G-BWFC	The helicopter was carrying oil rig workers to Shetland's Sumburgh Airport when a rotor transmission failure caused the helicopter to crash into the sea.
40	0	1948	KLM	Lockheed Constellation PH-TEN *Nijmegen*	En route to the United States, the aircraft was attempting to land at Prestwick Airport when it flew into high ground.
39	0	1948	Scandinavian Airlines System/RAF	Douglas DC-6 SE-BDA *Agnar Viking*/Avro York MW248	The two aircraft collided in mid-air over Northwood, London. It remains Britain's worst collision accident.[126]

UNDER BRIDGES

Some aviators have flown that bit more daringly than others, to 'push the envelope' that bit further. From the days of those early barnstormers who jumped from wing to wing, to the modern era, pilots have always been keen to show their skills. One of the most visible means of doing this has been to fly under bridges, or other man-made structures.

Tower Bridge, London

1912
Frank McClean flew his Short hydroplane through the gap between the road section and upper walkway. He then proceeded to fly under other bridges until he reached Westminster. He touched the water under Blackfriars Railway Bridge and on his return flight the following day his biplane was damaged when it came into contact with an obstruction on the water at Tower Bridge.

Brooklyn Bridge and Manhattan Bridge, New York, USA

1926

Viola Gentry gained the nickname the 'Flying Cashier' as she worked in a restaurant to help pay for her flying. She was the first woman to fly under both these New York bridges. Gentry set a solo endurance record in 1928 (circling Roosevelt Field in New York for 8 hours, 12 minutes) but a serious crash the following year hospitalised her for six months.[127]

Eiffel Tower

1944

Captain William Overstreet of the USAAF was chasing a Messerschmitt Me 109 over Paris in the spring of 1944 when the German pilot attempted to evade him by flying under the Eiffel Tower. In his P-51 Mustang *Berlin Express*, Overstreet followed him through the metal structure before shooting him down.[128]

Tower Bridge, London

1968

On 5 April 1968, Flight Lieutenant Alan Pollock took his Hawker Hunter fighter jet through the gap above the road as a protest against the lack of celebration for the RAF's 50th anniversary. Pollock was arrested after landing but was not court martialled. He was eventually discharged on medical grounds, a decision described by *Flight* magazine as 'strange'.

Winston Bridge, County Durham

1988

Famed display pilot Ray Hanna flew a Spitfire under this bridge for the TV series *Piece of Cake*. In order to keep a separation between his wings and the bridge's arch Hanna had to fly less than 20ft above the water.

UNUSUAL SHAPES IN THE SKY

Alexander Lippisch's Aerodyne

The Aerodyne was perhaps the oddest-looking machine of them all. It resembled a basking shark, its wide, circular fuselage wide open at the front to allow the encasement of its two contra-rotating propellers that provided lift by expelling air down through the fuselage. What added to its unusual design was the lack of wings.

Beluga

The Beluga – or Airbus A300-600ST Super Transporter – is one of the most unusual looking aircraft currently flying. Used to transport large component parts of Airbus airliners around Europe for final construction, the Beluga is a normal Airbus A300-600, but its cockpit section is lowered to below normal level. It ahas a large cylindrical cargo space mounted on top of the fuselage. It replaced the Boeing 'Super Guppies' which used the same format on a Stratocruiser airframe. The Beluga's space is larger than that available for cargo on the Antonov An-124, Boeing C-17 and Lockheed C-5A Galaxy: 23ft high by 23ft wide.

Blohm & Voss BV 141

This Second World War German reconnaissance aircraft was a monoplane with two wings, one engine, but only one tail plane and a short cockpit cabin that sat on the right-hand wing. Its asymmetric concept worked and it did fly.

Flying Bedstead

The 'Flying Bedstead' (actually called the Rolls-Royce Thrust Measuring Rig, although even official reports used its nickname) was an experimental machine to investigate control issues in an aircraft able to hover and take off and land vertically. The 'Flying Bedstead' was well named, as it resembled a piece of furniture more than an aircraft. It had no smooth exterior skin and aerodynamic drag was not an issue for a machine with such a limited flight profile. Its engines and associated pipes and nozzles were clearly visible, supported by four spindly undercarriage legs with castoring wheels at each corner. The pilot sat on top of the whole thing.

Two examples were built: one was severely damaged in an accident in September 1957 and the second was lost two months later, in an accident that killed the pilot.[129]

Lockheed XFV-1 Salmon and Convair XFY-1 Pogo

These aircraft, built in the early 1950s were 'tailsitters' – designed to take off and land vertically. They were to operate as ship defence aircraft, able to take off from ships that weren't aircraft carriers. Both were prototypes ordered by the US Navy to test the concept, although only the Pogo was able to take to the air vertically. It flew many test flights and was successfully landed each time. Safety considerations were made: the Convair's pilot was given 25ft of rope as an escape aid. Eventually the project was shelved as the navy focused on jet aircraft taking off conventionally from aircraft carriers for fleet protection.

McDonnell XF-85 Goblin

The egg-shaped Goblin was intended to be an escort fighter albeit with an unusual take off capability: it was to be carried inside the bomb bay of the long-range Convair B-36 bomber and then launched when required. Space restrictions meant it was the smallest jet fighter ever built at 14ft 10ins long. The effectiveness of the method of recovery – the Goblin carried a hook, which was to catch on a wire suspended below the bomber before being pulled up into the bomb bay – wasn't proven and it wasn't a capable enough fighter to challenge enemy aircraft. The advent of aerial refuelling spelled redundancy and the 'parasite fighter' project was abandoned.

Miles M.39B Libellula

This wartime British aircraft was a 'tail-first' design, configured with the pilot sitting very far forward, with one set of small wings below and in front of him. Two engines were hung underneath the swept-back rear wings, which ended with a tail fin each. A fuselage tail fin was positioned at the rear of the fuselage. A scale model was flown but the project was cancelled and the aircraft later broken up.

Nemuth Parasol

Built in 1834 the Parasol was exactly that: an aircraft with a wing completely circular as in the Parasol in shape. The Parasol was designed by students at Miami University.

Northrop YB-49

First flown in 1947, the YB-49 was a jet-powered development of the XB-35 propeller 'flying wing' aircraft, designed by Jack Northrop. With a wingspan of 172ft, it was a large aircraft, requiring eight J-35-A-5 engines to power it into the air. It was intended as a competitor for the strategic bomber contract but after the two prototypes were lost in accidents, the concept was not taken forward. It would take four decades for another flying wing bomber to fly and this one was to achieve air force procurement and a successful service career. One of the YB-49 prototypes broke up during a test flight, killing all on board. Among them was test pilot Glen W. Edwards. Muroc Air Force Base was renamed in his honour.

Vought V-173 'Flying Pancake'

Rather than the wing being circular the whole aircraft was circular, hence its nickname. The V-173 had two piston engines and was a 'tail-dragger'; sitting at an angle of 22 degrees. Glass panels were installed in the front of the fuselage/wing to allow the pilot a forward view of the ground. Its concept led to the VF5U 'Flying Flapjack'.

V IS FOR...

V-BOMBERS

Following the Second World War, the UK government issued requirements for a new long-range nuclear bomber able to attack targets inside the Soviet Union. Three different aircraft were selected as insurance, should any prove ineffective.

Type	First Flight	Max speed (mph)	Max altitude (ft)	Range (miles)	Number Built	Notes
Vickers Valiant	18 May 1951	567 (at 30,000ft)	54,000	4,500	107	The Valiant was the first V-bomber to enter RAF service (and saw action at Suez) but was also the first to be withdrawn in 1965 following wing spar metal fatigue problems.

Avro Vulcan	30 August 1952	645 *	60,000 *	4,600 *	136	World's first delta-winged heavy bomber. Could carry nuclear weapons or 21,000lb of conventional weapons. Used in Falklands War in 1982. Also operated as tanker. Retired in 1984.
Handley Page Victor	24 December 1952	640 (at 40,000ft) **	60,000 **	4,600 **	86	The B.2 version could carry 35 x 1,000lb conventional bombs. Switched to becoming aerial refuelling tanker role in mid-1960s. Retired from service in 1993.[130]

*Avro Vulcan B.2 version
**Victor B.2 version

VESNA VULOVIC

Vesna Vulovic gained her place in the record books on 26 January 1972 when she was working as cabin crew on a Yugoslav Airlines McDonnell Douglas DC-9. As the airliner passed over Czechoslovakia at 33,000ft it exploded. All of the crew and passengers were killed – except for the 23-year-old Vulovic who was found alive in the crashed tail section. She spent sixteen months in hospital and it was feared she would lose the ability to walk.

However, doubts have been expressed over the official account of the event that a Croatian terrorists' bomb blew the plane up. Investigative journalists have suggested that a Czech MiG fighter had shot it down at a much lower altitude. Whatever the speculation, Vulovic remains in the record books as surviving the highest fall without a parachute.

VICTOR TO THE SKY

The Cold War Jet Collection at the ex-RAF bomber base at Bruntingthorpe in Leicestershire is home to several aircraft from the Cold War. It is a museum with a difference in that some of these exhibits don't just sit gathering dust – although not certified to fly, they can carry out fast

Avro Vulcan XH558 at 2014 Scottish Airshow. (Norman Ferguson)

taxi runs. On 3 May 2009 ex-RAF tanker aircraft Handley Page Victor XM715 *Teasin' Tina* was lined up on the runway and the throttles pushed forward by ex-RAF Victor pilot Bob Prothero. The plan was to accelerate to 100 knots, pull the throttle back, and bring the aircraft to a stop. Unfortunately the retardation of the throttles wasn't done, and as XM715 continued to gain speed, Prothero had to take one of his hands off the control column to do this himself. In doing so, a degree of control was lost and the aircraft took to the air. It was immediately pushed sideways by a crosswind and after its 9-second flight Prothero was able to bring the V-bomber down safely, albeit on the grass beside the runway.

VOLCANO

Each aircraft in Icelandair's airline fleet is named after an Icelandic volcano:

Askja	*Hekla*	*Laki*
Búrfell	*Helgafell*	*Magni*
Eldborg	*Hengill*	*Skjaldbreiður*
Eldfell	*Herðubreið*	*Snæfell*
Eyjafjallajökull	*Katla*	*Snæfellsjökull*
Grábrók	*Keilir*	*Surtsey*
Grímsvötn	*Krafla*	*Öræfajökull*[131]

W IS FOR...

WESTRAY

Westray to Papa Westray is the world's shortest scheduled flight. The Loganair flight between the two Orkney islands takes less than 2 minutes.

WHAAM!

Whaam! is a 1963 painting by American pop artist Roy Lichtenstein. Based on comic book artwork, it shows an American P-51 Mustang firing a rocket at what appears to be an oncoming F-86 Sabre jet. The title comes from the onomatopoeic effect from the exploding fighter. Lichtenstein, who had served in the US Army during the Second World War, painted several other works with a military aeronautical theme, including *Jet Pilot* and *As I Opened Fire*.

WILLIAM REID

Glaswegian William Reid was a bomber pilot with 61 Squadron. His Lancaster was heading to Düsseldorf on 3 November 1943 when a German night fighter attacked it. Reid was subsequently wounded. Another fighter inflicted more damage, killing the navigator and wounding two other crewmen. Reid continued and the bomb-aimer, who knew nothing of the state of the crew or aircraft due to the failure of the aircraft's intercom system, carried out the attack. Reid then turned his stricken aircraft for home but was close to collapsing into unconsciousness from loss of blood. Eventually the airfield was sighted and he landed the Lancaster safely. Reid, who was 21 years old at the time, was given the highest award for valour available. The citation for his Victoria Cross award read:

> Wounded in two attacks, without oxygen, suffering severely from cold, his navigator dead, his wireless operator fatally wounded, his aircraft crippled and defenceless, Flight Lieutenant Reid showed superb courage and leadership in penetrating a further 200 miles into enemy territory to attack one of the most strongly-defended targets in Germany. His tenacity and devotion to duty were beyond praise.

He returned to active service with 617 Squadron and was shot down over Germany in 1944 when a bomb from another Lancaster hit his own aircraft. He was captured and spent the rest of the war in a prisoner-of-war camp. He died in 2001.

WIND-UP

In the First World War someone who had the 'wind-up' was deemed to be a nervous flyer. A windy flyer was not welcome, as it was feared their condition might be contagious and lessen overall morale.

WINTER FLYING

Winter Flying

Demands comfortably warm clothing and accessories. These bargains will help you forget the weather:

A-P Face Mask

This mask covers the entire face and chin. Removable mouth piece. Specially constructed nose feature permits free breathing. Tailored to last! Priced for clearance ... $2.50

Champagne Suede Helmet

This helmet is made of very soft suede and is known for its long wear and considered to be one of the most comfortable helmets. All seams are stitched with silk thread. Water proofed. Buy now at ... $1.75

Parachute Silk Scarf

Log book free with each scarf. Made of genuine white parachute silk. These scarfs are a handsome addition to any flyer's wardrobe. Attractive for dress as well as important part of equipment. Sale price only ... $1.38

Order Today!

Aviation Products Co, 619 S Federal St, Dept PA2, Chicago IL

Advert in *Popular Aviation* magazine, February 1937.

WOMEN AVIATORS

In the early years of aviation women pilots achieved much, despite opposition from some of their male counterparts who believed they couldn't achieve anything because of their gender. Despite their success they were often given nicknames in a manner that male pilots avoided. Ten of these were:

Daredevil Aviatrix
Daring Girl Bird
Dresden China Aviatrix
Flying Cashier
Flying Duchess
Flying Flapper
Flying Schoolgirl

Bessie Coleman
Julia Clark
Harriet Quimby
Viola Gentry
Mary Russell, Duchess of Bedford
Elinor Smith
Katherine Stinson

Harriet Quimby in Bleriot monoplane in 1911. (Library of Congress, Prints & Photographs Division, LC-USZ62-15070)

Girl Hawk   Hélène Dutrieu
Lady Lindy   Amelia Earhart
Tomboy of the Air   Blanche Scott[132]

WORKING AEROPLANES

In 1928's *The Big Book of Aeroplanes*, a chapter is devoted to 'Aeroplanes at work'. It describes the roles aircraft had been performing:

- Life-saving by the US coastguard service.
- Supplying food to cut off winter villages in Britain.
- Delivering mail across the English Channel.

- Protection of fishing stocks in Canada.
- Bombing fish (White Sturgeon) in France.
- Mapping unexplored parts of the world.
- Hunting seals in Canada.
- Chasing wolves from Siberian villages.

WRIGHT BROTHERS

Amos Root was the editor and publisher of the unlikely sounding aviation magazine *Gleanings in Bee Culture*. On 20 September 1904 Root was given the opportunity to spend time with the Wright brothers as they tested their latest flying machine, the Wright Flyer II, at the world's first aerodrome at Huffman Prairie, 8 miles from their home town of Dayton, Ohio.

The brothers were not keen on promotion, as they wished to protect their commercial secrets, but were happy to show their work to him. In the January edition of his magazine, Root printed his recollections, which included seeing the first complete circuit flown by a heavier-than-air flying machine:

> The engine is started and got up to speed. The machine is held until ready to start by a sort of trap to be sprung when all is ready; then with a tremendous flapping and snapping of the four-cylinder engine, the huge machine springs aloft. When it first turned that circle, and came near the starting-point, I was right in front of it; and I said then, and I believe still, it was one of the grandest sights, if not the grandest sight, of my life.

X IS FOR...

X SQUADRON

The original designation given to what became 617 Squadron when it was formed to carry out the Ruhr Dams raid of May 1943.

X-15

The North American X-15 was designed as a test vehicle for research into high speed and high altitude flight.

It was a short-winged craft powered by a single XLR-99 rocket engine, which delivered around 60,000lb of thrust. As it weighed around 33,000lb, when launched from its B-52 carrier aircraft the X-15 had a very good thrust-to-weight ratio and as fuel burned – reducing its weight to around 15,000lb – it resulted in a thrust-to-weight ratio of 4:1. Simply put: this made it very fast. At its fastest, it travelled 1.25 miles a second; it took only 6 seconds to go from Mach 5 to Mach 6.

Apollo astronaut Neil Armstrong, who flew the X-15 seven times, described it as 'the most successful research airplane in history' and it achieved some notable milestones and records during its nine years of flight:

Achievement	Details
First aircraft to reach Mach 4	Mach 4.43 on 7 March 1961
First aircraft to reach Mach 5	Mach 5.27 on 23 June 1961
First aircraft to reach Mach 6	Mach 6.04 on 9 November 1961
First aircraft to fly higher than 300,000ft	314,750ft reached on 17 July 1962
First aircraft to fly high enough to earn its pilots astronaut wings	Bob White on 17 July 1962
Highest altitude flown by aircraft	354,200ft on 22 August 1963[133]
Fastest aircraft ever built	Mach 6.7 (4,520mph) on 3 October 1967

X-15 being carried under a B-52 before launch. (NASA)

X-RAID PATROL

X-Raid – One destroyed by lucky burst. It blew up. Another did the same before I could open fire!

Logbook entry, 7 May 1941, Guy Gibson, 29 Squadron

X-Raids were incoming aircraft tracked by radar but not identified. They could be hostile or friendly and in order to investigate, air defence fighters were sent up. Gibson had volunteered to join Fighter Command and had been posted to 29 Squadron in late 1940. He shot down several German bombers in his period on night-fighters before returning to Bomber Command.

XF-11

The XF-11 was a prototype high-speed reconnaissance aircraft built by Howard Hughes. It was similar in layout to the P-38 Lightning with two-engines set at the front of twin tail booms, with the pilot sitting in a central fuselage. The XF-11's two engines powered four sets of contra-rotating propellers. The first flight was on 7 July 1946, the pilot Hughes himself. Once in the air he changed the flight plan and flew longer than the 20 minutes scheduled. During the flight an oil leak caused the right-hand engine to malfunction and Hughes attempted to land the aircraft on the Los Angeles Country Club golf course. He didn't make it and his descending aircraft struck houses in Beverley Hills. He was severely injured and the resultant treatment is said to have begun his addiction to painkillers. The US Air Force did not order the XF-11, although Hughes, following his recovery, successfully flew a second prototype in 1947.

XH558

XH558 was the world's last remaining flying Avro Vulcan until its retirement in 2015.

It first entered service with the RAF in 1960 and operated in the training and maritime reconnaissance roles before being converted to an aerial refuelling tanker. Following the type's retirement from squadron service in 1984, XH558 continued as a display aircraft with the RAF until 1992.

Before plans began to take shape on how to return it to flight by the Vulcan to the Sky Trust, XH558 was maintained at Bruntingthorpe where it performed taxiing runs. It took to the air again on 18 October 2007 and despite several technical issues that prevented some flights, XH558 was a popular addition to the airshow scene in the UK.

It flew for the last time in October 2015 following the withdrawal of the main technical support companies due to several issues, such as the decreasing level of knowledge about engine maintenance and the extra airframe hours the aircraft had accumulated beyond other Vulcans. During its time with the Trust it flew 228 times.

Y IS FOR...

YF-12

American manufacturer Lockheed had built the U2 spy plane and although it could reach high altitudes, it was slow and became vulnerable to the Soviet Union's surface-to-air missiles. A top-secret project was begun to find a replacement and in 1959 Lockheed were awarded the contract for a high-speed (Mach 3), high-altitude (90,000ft), long-range (4,000 miles) reconnaissance aircraft.

Under Project OXCART it began developing the A-12. The 'A' stood for 'Archangel' following from the name 'Angel' given to the U2 during its development for its customer, the CIA.

Discussions were had between Lockheed and the USAF on the aircraft's suitability as an interceptor and this was taken forward with the aircraft designated as the YF-12A. It had a two-man crew: a pilot and fire control officer who oversaw the Hughes AN/ASG-18 radar and three AIM-47 nuclear warhead missiles.

Missile firing tests were successful and the aircraft set world records for speed and altitude in May 1965 when an YF-12A reached 80,278ft and 2,070mph. However, the Secretary of Defence Robert McNamara cancelled the project in 1968 on cost-cutting grounds. NASA used two of the aircraft for high-speed tests.

The A-12 ended its operational life in 1968 but the USA had not lost its high-speed, high-altitude reconnaissance capability: the SR-71 Blackbird had began operations two years previously.

YF-12. (NASA)

YO-YO

The high yo-yo is an air combat manoeuvre where an attacking aircraft that is unable to remain behind an opponent – either through not being able to turn inside, or which has too much 'overtaking' speed – pulls up into the vertical, trading speed for height. It rolls over when inverted to track the opponent. By gaining altitude at the right moment the attacker has the advantage of being able to dive down and drop into a shooting position behind the opposing aircraft. The Low Yo-yo sees the attacker losing height in a turn to gain speed and close distance on the opponent before then climbing to lose speed and avoid over-shooting.

YURI GAGARIN

Gagarin became the first human to fly in space in April 1961 when he made one orbit of the Earth in *Vostok 1*. Much to his consternation, to the world's first cosmonaut was barred from making any more space flights as the Soviet authorities feared bad publicity if he died in an accident. He was allowed to fly aircraft but ironically died in a flying accident in March 1968. Mystery surrounded the circumstances that led to his death. The official version of events stated his aircraft had probably hit a weather balloon but this was countered by those such as cosmonaut Alexei Leonov who believed Gagarin's MiG 15 had been put into a tailspin by the wake of a passing Sukhoi Su 15 flying supersonically.

Z IS FOR...

ZA176

On 7 June 1983 Sub Lieutenant Ian 'Soapy' Watson was flying Sea Harrier ZA176 on a sortie off the coast of Portugal. When he decided to return to his aircraft carrier, HMS *Illustrious*, he found his navigation equipment and radio were not working properly. As he was too far from any diversion airfields Watson steered his aircraft towards shipping lanes with the intention of ejecting and being picked up by a nearby ship. When he spotted the Spanish container ship *Alraigo* he opted for another course of action something not taught in any flight manual and took his Sea Harrier for an improvised landing. He managed to land the vertical take-off and landing jet on top of the ship's containers. The aircraft was later recovered and returned to service. ZA176 had previous experience of being transported on such a ship; it had been transported to the Falklands in May 1982 on board the *Atlantic Conveyor*.[134]

ZEPPELIN

Born in 1838, Count Ferdinand von Zeppelin first flew in an observation balloon during the American Civil War and once back in Germany he became an advocate of using aerial craft for military purposes, but received no support.

He set about building and flying his own airships and the first (LZ.1) flew in 1900. In 1908 when one of his airships was badly damaged an influx of public donations (6 million marks) gave him the funds to set up a company based at Friedrichshafen.

Zeppelin's company built dirigibles for the Germany navy and their name became synonymous with the airship raiders who bombed Britain during the First World War, even though many of the attacking airships were built by Schütte-Lanz.

He founded the world's first commercial airline in 1909: Die Deutsche Luftschiffahrts Aktiengesellschaft (DELAG). The airline used seven airships and safely carried 34,000 passengers between 1910 and 1913.

Count von Zeppelin died in 1917, before the great airship that would carry his name, *Graf Zeppelin*, flew.

Graf Zeppelin (LZ.127)

At 776ft long it was the biggest in the world. On 15 October 1928 it made the first passenger flight over the Atlantic and the following year made the first airship flight around the world. It carried out flights to destinations in Europe and a scheduled service to South America. This giant of the skies

Graf Zeppelin flying over Berlin. (US Coast Guard)

also flew on a trip to the Arctic in 1931. However, following the *Hindenburg* disaster in 1937 the days of the large hydrogen-filled airship were not to last and *Graf Zeppelin* and its successor *Graf Zeppelin II* (LZ.130) were scrapped during the Second World War, their metal being used to build fixed-wing aircraft.[135]

ZERO

During the Second World War the Japanese navy's main fighter was the Mitsubishi A6M, called the Zero after its designation as the Type 0 Aircraft Carrier Fighter. (The '0' was due to the Imperial dating system which represented 1940 – the year the aircraft entered service – as 2600, shortened to '0'). It was an effective design, being light, armed with cannon, and able to fly long distances. American pilots were advised not to engage in dogfights with it at lower speeds. However it suffered in manoeuvrability at higher speeds and as it was made to be as light as possible, there was no armour plating. Another disadvantage for the pilot was the lack of self-sealing tanks, leading to more fires and explosions than with Allied aircraft. It was feared when first encountered but lost its position as the best naval fighter with the introduction of the American Hellcat in 1943.[136]

ZERO-ZERO EJECTION SEAT

The first ejection seat was used in an emergency on 30 May 1949 when Jo Lancaster ejected from an Armstrong-Whitworth AW52. This early type of seat had restrictions when it could be used, depending on the altitude, attitude and speed of the stricken aircraft. The developed zero-zero seat could be used at zero speed and zero altitude. It required the use of a rocket motor, to supplement the existing cartridge-fired ejection gun.

On 1 April 1961 Martin Baker employee W.T. Hay successfully tested the rocket-powered seat from ground level, reaching a speed of 90mph, raising him to a height of 300ft before he parachuted safely back to the ground. He repeated the demonstration at the 1961 Paris Air Show.[137]

ZERSTÖRER

The Messerschmitt Me 110 was the Luftwaffe's Zerstörer (Destroyer) – a heavy fighter intended to wreak havoc on any fighters that challenged the bomber formations it was escorting. The Me 110 was heavily armed with 2 x 20mm cannon and 5 x machine guns. The concept of a heavily armed, twin-engined fighter was not without merit, as the Mosquito, P-38 Lightning and P-61 Black Widow night-fighter later showed, but the 110 was too slow and unmanoeuverable when facing the nimble Spitfires and Hurricanes in the Battle of Britain. It was reduced to being escorted itself. When equipped with radar it became an effective night fighter, defending Germany against the Allied night bombing.

ZURABATIC CARTWHEEL

Janusz Zurakowski stunned onlookers at the 1951 Farnborough Airshow with this manoeuvre, which involved taking the two-engined Gloster Meteor into a vertical climb, then cutting the power on one engine to begin a flat 'swing'. As it descended the second engine was then cut and the cartwheel continued for oen and a half rotations.

The Polish-born Zurakowski had flown Spitfires in the Battle of Britain and shot down six German aircraft. He became a test pilot at Boscombe Down before joining Gloster. He moved to Canada where he flew the ill-fated Avro Arrow.

NOTES

1. http://www.thefirstairraces.net (5 February 2016)
2. Stenman, Kari; de Jong (translator), Peter *Fokker D.XXI Aces of World War 2* (Osprey Publishing, 2013)
3. http://www.aerobaticteams.net/raf-past-display-teams.html (5 February 2016); *Scale Aircraft Modelling*, November and December 2004
4. http://www.airbus.com/aircraftfamilies/passengeraircraft/a380family/ (5 February 2016)
5. Science Museum; http://www.australiangeographic.com.au/blogs/on-this-day/2012/05/on-this-day-darwin-applauds-record-flight (5 February 2016); http://www.museums.eastriding.gov.uk (5 February 2016); *Flight* (various)
6. Boyne, Walter *Boeing B-52 A Documentary History* (Jane's, 1981)
7. www.blueangels.navy.mil (5 February 2016)
8. http://www.boeing.com/history/ (5 February 2016)
9. http://www.456fis.org/ (5 February 2016)
10. http://www.niagarafallsinfo.com (5 February 2016); http://www.Lincolnbeachey.com (5 February 2016); http://www.nationalaviation.org/beachey-lincoln (5 February 2016); http://www.FrankMarrero.com (5 February 2016); Fisher, Scott M *Eastern Iowa's Aviation Heritage* (Arcadia Publishing, 2011)
11. Balch, Adrian M. *Airline Nostalgia. Classic Aircraft in Colour* (Airlife, 1999)
12. BBC; CD41 Recordings
13. *Guardian*, 24 October 2015
14. Thetford, Owen *Aircraft of the Royal Air Force since 1918* (Putnam, 1979)
15. *New Scientist*, 30 August 1984
16. Lancaster: McKinstry, Leo *Lancaster. The Second World War's Greatest Bomber* (John Murray, 2009); DC-3: http://www.boeing.com/news/frontiers/archive/2005/december/i_history.html (5 February 2016); F-16: Pace, Steve *X-Planes at Edwards* (MBI Publishing, 1995); Concorde: BBC; F-15: Ethell, Jeff *F-15 Eagle. Modern Combat Aircraft 12* (Ian Allan, 1981).
17. Global Market Forecast 'Flying on Demand 2014–2033' (Airbus, 2014)
18. *Wings of Fame*, Volume VIII (Aerospace Publishing Ltd, 1997)
19. Scott, Group Captain Desmond *Typhoon Pilot* (Leo Cooper, 1982)
20. http://www.phrases.org.uk/meanings/gordon-bennett.html (5 February 2016)
21. *Air & Space Magazine*, September 2006
22. Kessler, Lauren *The Happy Bottom Riding Club: The Life and Times of Pancho Barnes* (Random House, 2000)
23. V&A Museum; US National Park Service
24. British Newspaper Archive
25. BBC Wales

26. http://www.lockheedmartin.co.uk/us/100years/stories/hercules.html
     (5 February 2016); *Aircraft Illustrated*, September 1979
27. http://www.imdb.com (5 February 2016)
28. https://aviation-safety.net/ (5 February 2016); *Popular Mechanics*
29. Ellis, Paul *British Commercial Aircraft. Sixty Years in Pictures* (Jane's, 1980);
     Flight, 28 November 1946; *Flight*, 12 December 1946; *Flight*, 15 February
     1957; http://www.airhistory.org.uk (5 February 2016)
30. Endres, Gunter *British Aircraft Manufacturers since 1908* (Ian Allan, 1995)
31. Jenkins, Dennis R. *X-15 Extending the Frontiers of Flight* (NASA, 2007)
32. Van Wyngarden, Greg *'Richthofen's Circus': Jagdgeschwader Nr. 1*
     (Osprey 2004)
33. Zaloga, Steven J. *Kamikaze: Japanese Special Attack Weapons 1944–45*
     (Osprey, 2011)
34. *Daily Telegraph*, 13 October 2010
35. Ziegler, Mano *Rocket Fighter. The Story of the Messerschmitt Me 163*
     (Arms & Armour, 1976)
36. *Flight*, 29 May 1953
37. *The Times*, 10 August 1908; McCullough, David *The Wright Brothers*
     (Simon & Schuster, 2015)
38. *Flight*, 11 October 1957
39. Wood, Derek *Project Cancelled. The Disaster of Britain's Abandoned
     Aircraft Projects* (Tri-Service Press, 1975)
40. http://www.awm.gov.au (5 February 2016)
41. Aircraft Accident Report NTSB/AAR-10 /03 (National Transportation Safety
     Board, 2010)
42. *Air & Space Magazine*, September 2006
43. Simpson, Paul *The Mammoth Book of Air Disasters and Near Misses*
     (Robinson, 2014); Report on the accident to Boeing 777-236ER,
     G-YMMM, at London Heathrow Airport on 17 January 2008 (Air Accidents
     Investigation Branch, 2010)
44. Battle of Britain Memorial Flight; *Daily Telegraph*, 29 March 1968
45. *Yorkshire Post*; Howard, Bill *What the RAF Airman Took to War*
     (Shire Publications, 2015); http://www.rafmuseum.org.uk/cosford
     (5 February 2016)
46. *Flight*, 23 January 1964; *Flight*, 23 December 1911; *Flight*,
     30 September 1911
47. *Montreal Gazette*, 19 July 1927
48. Kaplan, Philip *Big Wings: The Largest Aeroplanes Ever Built* (Pen &
     Sword, 2005)
49. http://www.raf.mod.uk/ (5 February 2016)
50. *Breverton's First World War Curiosities* by Terry Breverton (Amberley
     Publishing, 2014)
51. Sturtivant, Ray *The History of Britain's Military Training Aircraft*
     (Haynes, 1987)
52. *Flight*, 8 February 1945
53. *Flight*, 23 June 1949
54. Penrose, Harald *British Aviation. The Pioneer Years 1903–1914*
     (Cassell, 1967)

55. Gibbs-Smith, Charles H. *The Invention of the Aeroplane 1799–1909* (Faber and Faber, 1966)

56. *Flight*, 8 January 1915; Roe, Sir Alliott Verdon *The World Of Wings And Things* (1939)

57. The 9/11 Commission Report (National Commission on Terrorist Attacks Upon the United States, 2004)

58. Orlebar, Christopher *The Concorde Story* (Osprey, 1997)

59. www.spitsbergeb-Svalbard.com (5 February 2016); www.frammuseum.no (5 February 2016)

60. *Huffington Post*, 11 March 2014

61. *International Business Times*, 20 March 2014

62. *NY Daily News*, 18 February 2011

63. *Daily Telegraph*, 10 July 2002

64. *Huffington Post*, 3 January 2013

65. *Daily Telegraph*, 19 March 2014

66. *International Business Times*, 20 March 2014

67. *Metro*, 3 February 2009

68. *Daily Telegraph*, 6 May 2009

69. *International Business Times*, 20 March 2014

70. *Flypast*, November 2014; *Flight*, 9 August 1945; *Flight*, 27 April 1912; *Flight*, 27 September 1913; Fédération Aéronautique Internationale.

71. Cobham plc; RAF Museum

72. Weal, John *Jagdgeschwader 51 'Mölders'* (Osprey, 2006)

73. *Air & Space Magazine*, 30 June 2012; *Flight*, 13 October 1938

74. Lepage, Jean-Denis G.G. *Aircraft of the Luftwaffe, 1935–1945: An Illustrated Guide* (McFarlane & Company, 2009)

75. NASA

76. Bowman, Martin W. *Mosquito Bomber/Fighter-Bomber Units 1942–45* (Osprey, 1997)

77. http://www.usmarshals.gov/history/fist/airlines.htm (5 February 2016)

78. *Air Force Times*; *Air International*, January 2011

79. *Flight*, 1 October 1942

80. http://www.nationalaviation.org/quimby-harriet (5 February 2016); PBS

81. Anderson, John D. *A History of Aerodynamics: And Its Impact on Flying Machines* (Cambridge University Press, 1998)

82. Seddon, John M.; Newman, Simon *Basic Helicopter Aerodynamics* (John Wiley & Sons, 2011)

83. Lebow, Eileen F. *Before Amelia: Women Pilots in the Early Days of Aviation* (Potomac Books, 2002)

84. Harding, John *Flying's Strangest Moments: Extraordinary But True Stories from Over 1,100 Years of Aviation History* (Pavilion Books, 2015)

85. *New York Herald*, 6 October 1908

86. Gibbs-Smith, Charles H. *The Invention of the Aeroplane 1799–1909* (Faber and Faber, 1966)

87. Turner, Charles Cyril *The Romance of Aeronautics. An Interesting Account of the Growth Achievements of All Kinds of Aerial Craft* (Seeley, Service & Co., 1912)

88. *Flying*, November 1957

89.   *Reaching for the Skies* (BBC TV, 1988)
90.   'Expectation and Reality. The Great War in the Air' by John H. Morrow Jnr in *Airpower Journal*, Winter 1996
91.   *Oxford Essential Quotations* (OUP, 2015)
92.   National Archives
93.   *Sydney Morning Herald*, 8 August 1930
94.   Churchill, Winston S. *The World Crisis Volume III: 1916–1918* (Bloomsbury, 2015)
95.   http://digital.library.unlv.edu/hughes/xf11.php (February 2016)
96.   *Daily Mail*, 17 June 1919
97.   www.frammuseum.no (5 February 2016)
98.   'Higher, Faster' *Flypast*, November 2014
99.   *Flight*, 14 & 28 August, 4 September 1909
100. Mackersey, Ian *No Empty Chairs: The Short and Heroic Lives of the Young Aviators Who Fought and Died in the First World War* (Hachette, 2012)
101. Gibson, Guy *Enemy Coast Ahead* (Crecy Publishing, 2006)
102. http://www.historynet.com/deadly-sabre-dance.htm (5 February 2016)
103. http://www.aviation-history.com/airmen/andree.htm (5 February 2016)
104. *Air & Space Magazine*, September 2012
105. *Air & Space Magazine*, 31 May 1988; http://www.RJ Mitchell-spitfire.co.uk (5 February 2016)
106. Levine, Joshua *Forgotten Voices of the Blitz and the Battle of Britain* (Ebury Press, 2007)
107. Levine, Joshua *Forgotten Voices of the Blitz and the Battle of Britain* (Ebury Press, 2007)
108. Price, Alfred *Spitfire. A Complete Fighting History* (Promotional Reprint Company 1991)
109. Crook, Flight Lieutenant David *Spitfire Pilot. A Personal Account of the Battle of Britain* (Greenhill Books, 2006)
110. McKinstry, Leo *Spitfire: Portrait of a Legend* (John Murray, 2008)
111. Spitfire documentary (BBC, 1976)
112. Price, Alfred *Spitfire. A Complete Fighting History* (Promotional Reprint Company 1991)
113. Gilman, Richard *Angels Ten! Memoirs of a WWII Spitfire Pilot* (Friesen Press, 2012)
114. *Spitfire* (Documentary) (BBC, 1976)
115. *Battle Stations: Spitfire Squadron* (War History Documentary) (History Channel 2000)
116. Chalke Valley History talk (June 2015)
117. *Spitfire Ace. First of the Few* (RDF Media/Channel 4, 2004)
118. Kershaw, Tim *Jet Pioneers. Gloster and the Birth of the Jet Age* (Sutton Publishing, 2004)
119. Alliance for Downtown New York, press release, 23 July 2012
120. Winslow, T.E. *Forewarned is Forearmed. A History of the Royal Observer Corps* (William Hodge & Company, 1948)
121. Lea, Flight Lieutenant Rob *Display Pilot. Flying the RAF's Combat Aircraft* (Osprey, 1994)
122. *Flight*, 12 December 1958

123. *Global News*; *Seattle Times*
124. F-35 JOINT STRIKE FIGHTER Assessment Needed to Address Affordability Challenges, Report to Congressional Committees, April 2015
125. US National Naval Aviation Museum
126. Simpson, Paul *The Mammoth Book of Air Disasters and Near Misses* (Robinson, 2014); https://aviation-safety.net (5 February 2016)
127. Bower, Jennifer Bean *North Carolina Aviatrix Viola Gentry: The Flying Cashier* (Arcadia, 2015)
128. http://www.warbirdsnews.com/ (5 February 2016)
129. Illingworth, J.K.B. *Flight Tests of a Hovering Jet-Lift Aircraft* (Rolls-Royce Flying Bedstead) (HMSO, 1963)
130. Thetford, Owen *Aircraft of the Royal Air Force since 1918* (Putnam, 7th Ed, 1979)
131. http://www.icelandair.co.uk (5 February 2016)
132. Mitchell, Charles R.; House, Kirk W. *Flying High: Pioneer Women in American Aviation* (Arcadia, 2002)
133. NASA; Jenkins, Dennis R. *X-15 Extending the Frontiers of Flight* (NASA, 2007); Thompson, Milton O. *At the Edge of Space: The X-15 Flight Program* (Smithsonian Institution, 1992)
134. *Air & Space Magazine*, November 2008;
15. http://www.airships.net (5 February 2016); Richards, John *A History of Airships* (The History Press, 2009)
136. Pacific Aviation Museum; Bergerud, Eric M. *Fire in the Sky: the Air War in the South Pacific* (Basic Books, 2001)
137. *Flight*, 13 April 1961; http://www.martin-baker.com/ (5 February 2016)